Deconstructing Conflict

Deconstructing Conflict

Understanding Family Business, Shared Wealth and Power

Doug Baumoel
Blair Trippe

CONTINUITY MEDIA
DeconstructConflict.com

Published by Continuity Media
100 Cummings Center, Suite 405D
Beverly, MA 01915

ISBN: 978-0996425612

First edition: 2016

The following terms are all trademarks of Continuity LLC: The Conflict Equation, Deconstructing Conflict, Family Factor, and Releasing Blame.

Praise for *Deconstructing Conflict*™

"In *Deconstructing Conflict*, Doug Baumoel and Blair Trippe uncover the true sources of conflict in family businesses. They show us that our amorphous anxieties are the result of systematic underlying influences that can be understood and managed. If you've ever been caught in the devastating undertow of conflict, this book offers hope and a way back to shore."

Doug Stone
Author, *Difficult Conversations: How to Discuss What Matters Most*

"Conflict is an inevitable part of life and business. When they intersect, as they do in family businesses, it is essential to anticipate and deal with problems, so that family relationships can thrive and the business succeed. *Deconstructing Conflict* is an indispensable guide that outlines the perils and benefits of family business systems, and offers practical and wise advice for keeping those systems intact."

Susan Hackley
Managing Director, Program on Negotiation, Harvard Law School

"Doug Baumoel and Blair Trippe give those of us committed to multi-generational family enterprises a roadmap for survival. Taking a systems approach and recognizing the unique importance of continuing relationships in family enterprises, they help us understand the challenges and keys to success in managing conflict. *Deconstructing Conflict* explains why structural and personal development is the best approach to growing the enterprise out of conflict. Baumoel and Trippe give family enterprise leaders and advisors the strategies and tools necessary for resolving conflict and sustaining their family enterprises."

Lansing Crane
Sixth-generation retired Chair and CEO, Crane & Co.

"All families have conflicts, but conflicts within family businesses can be debilitating and have far-reaching consequences – not only on the family but on employees, customers, suppliers, and providers of capital. *Deconstructing Conflict* is an incredibly smart and accessible read for anyone grappling with a conflict. It is a useful, timely, and practical guide for all family businesses that have faced, or will face, some form of conflict. As Doug and Blair state, the purpose of conflict resolution is not to eliminate conflicts, but to comprehend and manage them. This is a must-read for any family business, and for all families facing conflict."

Partha Bose
Partner and Chief Marketing Officer, International Strategy Consulting Firm, and Author of *Alexander the Great's Art of Strategy: Lessons from the Great Empire Builder*

"Doug Baumoel and Blair Trippe have created an exceptionally useful guide to understanding and managing the complex matrix of family business conflict. Family business consultants, mediators, and family business owners will all benefit from the wealth of insight and experience captured in these pages."

David A. Hoffman, Esq.
John H. Watson Jr. Lecturer on Law, Harvard Law School, and Founder of the Boston Law Collaborative, LLC

"*Deconstructing Conflict* is a comprehensive analysis of the prevalent yet painful issue of conflict in family enterprises. Like most other aspects of wealthy families or families in business, the conflicts that arise are marked by their inherent complexity. Doug Baumoel and Blair Trippe wade into this complexity with skill, intelligence, and experience. At the center of the book is their *Conflict Equation*, a thoughtful exposition of the core components of family conflict and how those components interact. Their methodical approach to explaining, and helping families move beyond, conflict is an invaluable addition to the field. I highly recommend it for families of wealth, family businesses, and the advisors who work with them."

James Grubman, PhD
FamilyWealth Consulting, Author of *Strangers in Paradise: How Families Adapt to Wealth Across Generations*, and co-author of *Cross Cultures: How Global Families Negotiate Change Across Generations*

"Conflict is a key reason why family businesses fail to succeed to the next generation. When properly managed, however, conflict can actually strengthen the family and ensure that both the family and business remain healthy. *Deconstructing Conflict* draws from research rooted in conflict management and family psychology to help enterprising families understand their idiosyncratic sources of conflict. This book offers the tools to better understand sources of conflict and to then develop individualized plans of action that take into account a family's unique values, relationships, and history. Whether a family business is currently suffering from conflict or hopes to avoid future conflicts, *Deconstructing Conflict* is an important resource."

Kimberly A. Eddleston, PhD
Professor of Entrepreneurship and Innovation at Northeastern University's D'Amore-McKim School of Business

"Using the methodology described in *Deconstructing Conflict*, Doug and Blair educated my family about concepts and principles inherent in all family businesses, and then helped us to develop and apply the tools necessary to optimally manage the needs of our business and family. I am forever indebted to them for their commitment and invaluable expertise. I expect that others reading this book will feel the same way."

Tom Swan III
Co-CEO, The Swan Group

"Conflict in family business is unavoidable, and tends to compound over generations. The ability of stakeholders to manage that conflict is the single most important challenge for any family that works or owns together. *Deconstructing Conflict* provides needed insight to truly understand what is going on in enterprising families, and details a fascinating method for tackling conflict so the potential family enterprise can be realized. With clarity, Doug and Blair illustrate how such a complex force can be taken apart piece by piece, showing families a way to put themselves back together."

Eric Allyn
Fourth-generation former Owner and Chairman, Welch Allyn Inc.

"Everyone has observed and encountered conflict in a business family that destroys business and personal relationships in about equal measure. There is a sense of helplessness about what to do, but Doug and Blair offer their model and roadmap for how a family, with an advisor, can move productively to identify and manage the key issues. *Deconstructing Conflict* is well-organized, comprehensive, and most of all, it offers clear steps for a family to move into productive engagement, even when differences have been allowed to develop for a long time without effective intervention. I'm grateful to have it to guide my own work with families, and to help me navigate this most universal and challenging area of practice."

Dennis Jaffe, PhD
Organizational Consultant and Clinical Psychologist

"Blair and Doug have tapped into the essence of family business: the range of emotions, the actors, the simplicity, the complexity. While many books address the topic of conflict in family business, which is often seen as ubiquitous, Blair and Doug have examined not only its construct, but how conflict can be managed. Conflict is not something to be eliminated but understood deeply, from both the advisor's perspective and, more importantly, from the perspective of each individual stakeholder. *Deconstructing Conflict* delivers!"

Daniel G. Van Der Vliet
The John and Dyan Smith Executive Director of Family Business, Smith Family Business Initiative, Cornell University

Dedications

To Victoria, Emily, and William for indulging my passion for this work;
To my parents for providing me the experiences on which to draw; and
To my mentor, the late Dr. Léon Danco, for helping me combine the two.

- Doug Baumoel

To Tory and Brian, the stars in my sky.

-Blair Trippe

Contents

Foreword

I have spent the last twenty-five years working with leaders around the world who have struggled to lead their countries from dictatorship to democracy and from conflict to peace. Using the shared human experience approach, which I developed with my colleagues in the early 1990s, we bring leaders together with those who have previously led transitions in other countries to share their firsthand experience. Our belief is that people can learn from the experience of others, and seeing that leaders similar to themselves overcame once-intractable problems provides them with the courage and tools to lead positive change in their own country and community.

Using this approach, we have supported leaders in Central and Eastern Europe and the former Soviet Union as they confronted the legacy of seventy years of Communist rule and repression, helped South Africans create their Truth and Reconciliation Commission in the aftermath of apartheid, helped leaders in Northern Ireland imagine the possibility of peace, and worked to promote reconciliation in the aftermath of war in Central America and the Balkans. Most recently, we helped set the conditions for the breakthrough between Cuba and the United States after six decades of polarization, and continue to promote reconciliation between both countries.

The shared human experience approach has proven to be a powerful and transformative model for change because it is founded on the recognition that individuals, no matter where they live, no matter their race, ethnicity, religion or gender, can learn from the experience of others who have struggled to overcome deep-seated fear and division, and through those examples develop the capacity to lead positive change themselves.

Through my work, I have come to recognize that there are fundamental drivers of conflict and reconciliation that exist at the national, international and personal levels. Drivers that are not defined by culture, ethnicity or geography, but are instead driven by the universal human need to be acknowledged, understood, and validated as one sees oneself. My experience shows that all conflict – whether at the national or personal level – is driven by exclusion, by the experience of being marginalized and ignored; failing to recognize and acknowledge the identity of others as they see themselves. Individuals and communities have a longing and a need to be included and to be agents of their own future and success. In fact, neuroscientists using brain-imaging technology have found that we experience social rejection as physical pain in the brain. The region of the brain that processes trauma cannot fully differentiate between emotional and physical trauma.

When I learned about the important work of Blair and Doug, I immediately recognized that many of the same dynamics that drive conflict and promote reconciliation around the world are fundamentally the same drivers of conflict and reconciliation within families and family-owned businesses experiencing identity-based conflict. This comes as no surprise. Humans are wired the same way no matter where they live or what they do. Our survival as a species depended on feeling safe and secure, which is deeply tied to feeling understood, to be acknowledged as you see yourself and not as others see you, and to be included in decisions about your own future. These deep and basic human needs are the root of conflict and reconciliation, whether on the global stage or, as Blair and Doug point out in *Deconstructing Conflict*, in identity-based conflicts where continuing relationships matter in families who need to share and work together effectively. Efforts to achieve peace in Northern Ireland and peacefully end apartheid in South Africa succeeded when all parties, even the smallest and most marginalized, were brought to a table where the dominant parties did not impose their will, and when communities felt they had agency over their own future – in short, where they felt acknowledged, valued, and safe.

In this wonderful and important book, Blair and Doug address several key themes that drive identity-based conflict and reconciliation within families — themes that I have seen in my own work globally. Families that have owned businesses for several generations often fight over legacies, cling to narratives of loss and humiliation, and show an unwillingness to compromise over values they hold deeply.

In my work I have seen conflict deepen when individuals and communities fight over which person or community is the greater victim. Groups who have experienced great loss and trauma often cannot move forward until their loss is acknowledged by others. I have seen leaders of the Cuban-American community move towards reconciliation and healing when their deeply felt sense of loss and trauma, experienced in the aftermath of the Cuban Revolution, was acknowledged and validated by leaders on all sides of the divide.

Neuroscientists and social psychologists have also done important and groundbreaking work on several fronts, including powerful research on sacred values. Sacred values are those values that are above compromise and are key to our identity and sense of place in the world. Research shows, and neuroimaging now confirms, that we process those values we hold as sacred – our children, the principles of our religion, family honor – in different regions of the brain than more utilitarian or transactional thoughts. The research shows that when we are asked to compromise our sacred values, we hold on to them more deeply and respond with anger and aggression. It is only when others recognize our sacred values that we begin to listen. When we don't feel under threat, we are able to listen to the other side rationally and begin the process of healing and reconciliation.

Conflict and reconciliation within family-owned companies is no different than conflict and reconciliation around the world. It begins with acknowledging our shared humanity, our common need to be heard, understood and included in fundamental decisions that shape our future. The South African transition was enshrined in the new South African Constitution, which recognized the inviolate dignity of all its citizens and offered gestures of respect towards what was sacred to others. No South African will ever forget the moment when Nelson Mandela, attending the World Cup game in Durban, donned the green cap of the Springboks, the rugby team that defined the Afrikaner community for generations. That symbolic moment signaled to the white community that peace and reconciliation was possible, and stripped any sense of shame from the community that imprisoned Mandela for nearly thirty years.

I hope that you, the reader, find *Deconstructing Conflict* as illuminating and powerful as I found it, and that whether you are in Belfast, Boston, or a family business, it helps you in addressing your own challenges.

Timothy Phillips, co-founder and CEO of Beyond Conflict

Acknowledgements

We would like to acknowledge our clients, and the following people who have influenced our thinking and whose support has been influential in writing this book:

Eric Allyn, Peter Begalla, Partha Bose, Urie Bronfenbrenner, Jill Carin Adams, Lanse Crane, John Davis, Sam Davis, Michael Dues, Charles Dwyer, Kim Eddleston, Paul Faxon, Sandi Geller, Judy Green, Meta Greenberg, Jim Grubman, Susan Hackley, David Hoffman, Jay Hughes, Dennis Jaffe, Arline Kardasis, Dennis Kessler, Rikk Larsen, Donella Meadows, Susan Mercurio, Kathy O'Hara, Tim Phillips, Larry Posner, Bertrand Raven, Bette Roth, Carl Sagan, Jay Shetterly, Robert Spitzer, Janis Abrahms Spring, Ron Stetler, Art Stewart, Doug Stone, Ron Sweet, Brian Trippe, Dann van der Vliet, Terry Windhorst, and Jack Wofford.

Thank you also to our book team: editing by Kate Victory Hannisian of Blue Pencil Consulting; book cover and layout by Jenny Putnam of J. Putnam Design; and proofreading by Nancy Baumoel.

Chapter 1

Introduction and Foundational Concepts

We cannot destroy kindred: our chains stretch a little sometimes, but they never break.
— Marquise de Sévigné

It is unlikely that you know of a conflict-free family business. There are certainly plenty that operate smoothly or that have warm or close family members, but one that has no conflict would be close to impossible. With over 85% of American businesses being family-owned and operated, and an even higher percentage in many other countries around the world, we wrote this book to explain to stakeholders and their advisors the nature of conflict in family business and how it can be managed successfully. After all, conflict inevitably impacts most family businesses and can have devastating consequences for its stakeholders.

In this book, we not only deconstruct conflict into its component parts, we also show how each of these components interacts and what can be done to keep conflict from escalating and damaging both the family and its enterprise. Only by fully understanding why the potential for conflict is so high in family business systems, and what the underlying causes and triggers for conflict are, can these conflicts be managed successfully.

This book introduces *The Conflict Equation*™, a powerful tool we developed to help make sense of what is going on in the conflicts that challenge stakeholders of an enterprising family. It guides users to successfully manage outright conflict, prevent unintended conflict and get un-stuck when they are paralyzed by fear of conflict.

The Conflict Equation was developed over fifteen years of working with scores of families sharing ownership of businesses and assets ranging in size from millions to billions of dollars. Although *The Conflict Equation* was developed for family businesses and enterprising families of significant size and complexity, the methods presented in this book also apply to smaller businesses. It is an approach that can be applied in the boardroom just as easily as it can be used around the dining room table.

Conflict in family enterprise is a type of identity-based, systemic conflict among stakeholders who share important continuing relationships that must survive the conflict. Seen through this lens, conflict in a family business has more in common with ethnic, political, and religious conflict than it does with the non-family, civil disputes we experience and read about daily.

This is a book about understanding and managing conflict in *family enterprise*. However, as we explain in this book, family business conflict, or conflict over shared wealth, is just one example of a broader category of conflict: identity-based, systemic conflict among stakeholders who share important continuing relationships that must survive the conflict. Seen through this lens, conflict in a family business has more in common with ethnic, political, and religious conflict than it does with the kind of non-family, civil disputes we experience and read about daily.

We will dive into just what this means shortly, but it is useful to take this perspective with you as you read this book: Studying conflict in a family enterprise is the perfect crucible for better understanding many of the global conflicts that seem intractable. The methods described here are equally applicable to this broader constellation of conflicts. Conversely, we can learn a lot about managing conflict in a family business from finding out what works (and what doesn't work) in managing political and ethnic conflict on the world stage. It is with this perspective that we designed the methodology described in this book.

There is much to digest in this book and some readers will know more than others about certain topics. Accordingly, we invite you to peruse the headings and skip subjects with which you may already be familiar or that provide more detail than you would like.

Why a book devoted to understanding and managing conflict in family businesses? Conflicts in family business make headlines in our newspapers, prompt exposés in our business journals, and are the subject of popular books and movies. The bigger the business, the more sensational the story! However, poorly managed conflict can be the most devastating threat to family businesses of any size. Yet despite the prevalence of conflict in a family business, most family stakeholders and advisors do not truly understand the special nature of this type of conflict and are thus typically unprepared to manage these conflicts when they strike.

When family dynamics combine with management, ownership and economic interests, the resulting mix can prove exponentially more complex. This is especially true when conflict erupts. How can business-related conflict be managed in a situation where the parties involved can't simply quit and start somewhere else? How can a conflict situation be worked out when these relationships are so important and uniquely permanent (i.e., siblings, cousins, parent, child)? How can family members with different values and interests share and manage assets together through generations? How can what's "fair" be agreed upon across all interest groups – when many of the issues in play are of crucial importance to stakeholders?

Through our extensive work with family firms and families who share significant wealth, we have found not only that conflict is inherent in these organizations, but also that *how conflict is managed* is often the difference between success and failure for these families and their enterprises. We have identified that the type of conflict inherent in family enterprise is poorly understood and that to be truly effective, family business stakeholders and their advisors must gain a better understanding of this type of conflict and be trained in effective approaches for its management.

The Conflict Equation is the synthesis of our experience working with families mired in some of the most extreme conflicts. This approach takes into account these five foundational concepts:

1. The potential for conflict is built into the structure of family enterprises.
2. How conflict is managed is central to the success or failure of the family business system.
3. These conflicts strike at the heart of stakeholder identities.

4. These conflicts exist among people whose continuing relationships are important, and these continuing relationships must be considered at every stage of a conflict management effort.

5. Conflict cannot be understood and managed by separating substantive from emotional issues. Rather, these conflicts must be managed in a way that integrates both the substantive or economic interests at hand as well as the personal and relationship factors in play *simultaneously*.

The Conflict Equation was originally developed as a framework for our own family business consulting work with clients to ensure that we thoroughly understood what was needed for clients to move forward — typically, through difficult and challenging conflict — and that we were able to develop comprehensive solutions for them that were reliable and effective. The method was developed, therefore, for the consultant's use, not the client's.

In the process of applying this method with scores of clients, however, we found that clients gained enormous value from learning the methods *themselves* and were able to apply these concepts for the long term. That said, learning how to deconstruct conflict can be exceedingly helpful, but there are limits to what a family member or other stakeholder in the system can accomplish as conflict managers within their own conflict situation. Having a stake in the outcome makes objectivity difficult; therefore, incorporating a neutral professional can add immeasurably to the success of the process.

This book, and *The Conflict Equation* methodology it describes, will help you — the stakeholder or advisor in a family enterprise — deconstruct conflict into its component parts, understand what triggers active conflict, and learn how to help all stakeholders manage these conflicts. In doing so, you will be armed with the most effective tool for achieving generational success in your, or your client's, family enterprise.

Why Is This So Important?

Family businesses are the backbone of the world's economy. Sixty percent of the US Gross National Product (GNP) comes from family businesses, and family businesses are responsible for over 90% of all new job creation in the US. Around the world, family business often plays an even stronger role in local and national economies. While statistics vary widely, and are not relevant when you are only concerned about one specific business (i.e., yours), we provide some here to help put into perspective just how important family businesses are to the world's economy.

It is clear that these statistics include many very small family businesses. In fact, many people think that family firms are de facto small businesses. However, some of the largest and most successful companies are family-controlled companies. Fully one-third of the S&P 500 firms are family owned, run or controlled in some fashion. Household names like Walmart, Fidelity, Nike, Toyota, Novartis, and Samsung are family-owned and controlled businesses.

You may have heard the proverb "shirtsleeves to shirtsleeves in three generations," implying that the first generation creates the wealth, the second generation preserves the wealth, and the third generation squanders the wealth. While there is some historical truth to this, we think it oversimplifies the situation and that families who can successfully manage the conflicts inherent in sharing wealth and power can break this cycle to develop productive, multigenerational approaches for sharing and building wealth.

There is a related admonition often quoted in family business literature that only one-third of all family businesses successfully transition to the next generation. By this logic, only about 10% make it to the third generation – a clear parallel to the shirtsleeves proverb. This is a misleading myth as it implies that the other 90% "fail." The fact is that family businesses are indeed excellent ways for families to build wealth and influence through many generations.

This unfortunate statistic was derived from a very limited study of family businesses many years ago and is often used to imply that at any given time, fully two-thirds of all family businesses will "fail" to transition, and thus be considered "failed" family businesses. The statistic misrepresents reality because many family businesses simply may not have been built with the intention to transition their businesses to future generations. Some families, for example, choose to sell their businesses due to market pressures or just because the right price is offered. For very small businesses — so-called *lifestyle businesses* that exist solely for the purpose of sustaining a particular family lifestyle for its current generation of stakeholders — growth and succession planning are generally not central concerns. Finally, there just may not be any heirs interested in taking over the business, thus prompting the company's sale and potentially providing the family with significant resources to do other things.

The point is that a failure to transition a business to the next generation may not be a "failure" after all. All businesses face market risks – even non-family firms fail or get bought out. The real question is: *Are family firms less successful than non-family firms?* The answer to this, according to many research sources, is a resounding "no." Family firms are generally more successful than their non-family counterparts in longevity and long-term profitability. This is due in large part to their long-term outlook, retention of talented employees, and lack of pressure from shareholders driven by short-term financial goals. All these statistics mean nothing, however, when the only business you are interested in is *yours*.

> The tragedy is when family businesses fail to transition to new leaders and owners due to poor planning or poorly managed conflict.

Not all families plan to transition their businesses to a next generation, and there are many good reasons why individual enterprises don't transition. The tragedy is when family businesses fail to transition to new leaders and owners due to poor planning or poorly managed conflict. It is clear to us that families who can manage the particular types of conflict that exist when families own or work together can dramatically improve their chances of transitioning wealth and business opportunity through the generations. When conflict is managed well, it paves the way for better, more proactive planning – further supporting multigenerational success.

Understanding Some Key Terms in This Book

Defining Conflict

As mentioned above, conflict in a family business, or within a family of generational wealth, is systemic. This means that conflict is built into the organizational structures that connect the family to its enterprise or wealth. These conflicts also are identity-based, meaning that the issues surrounding these conflicts typically speak to strongly held, self-defining values, beliefs and roles.

Because of these complicating factors, conflict in a family business is distinct from common civil disputes and does not typically respond to the same dispute resolution approaches (e.g., litigation, mediation) that might be considered when unrelated parties fight over economic issues or over power and control.

Another distinguishing factor in family business conflict is that the continuing family relationships are very important and must survive the conflict. Stakeholders typically cannot just compromise and walk away. They must find a way to remain "family" after the fight. Therefore, family relationships must be considered at every stage of the conflict management process. *The Conflict Equation* does exactly this – throughout the process it considers individual and group relationships, how they have developed over time, and what family members want in the future.

Conflict in family enterprise is also very different from the strictly personal grudges and arguments that develop in families over emotional and relationship issues. When these issues are coupled with economic issues and issues of who holds power and how power is used in the family and in its shared enterprise, family therapy and psychology alone simply cannot provide robust solutions to these complex and intense situations. Decisions in business often cannot wait for psychological change to take place – even if change would be beneficial.

Trying to separate substantive economic issues from emotional and relationship-based issues, so they might be tackled independently, often proves counterproductive. Instead, economic, emotional, and relationship issues are locked together in family enterprise and must be addressed in an integrated and comprehensive manner. *The Conflict Equation* methodology offers such an approach.

Active and Passive Conflict

The term "conflict," as we use it in this book, not only concerns active, visible battles among stakeholders where the cause of the disputes is clear and battle lines are clearly drawn. The kind of conflict that we are concerned with also includes subtler manifestations, such as:

- Being stuck and unable to move forward due to fear that conflicts might be triggered if important decisions are made, or needed actions are taken;

- Tensions and bias handed down from previous generations that limit the enterprise;
- Structural pitfalls designed to avoid conflict like siloing and the lack of accountability systems;
- Tacit disagreement about how power is shared and used;
- Factionalism among family branches;
- Disrespect and friction among stakeholders;
- Lack of alignment concerning strategy and tactics;
- Uncertainty spawned by poor planning; and
- Crisis due to unexpected events, market changes, and/or competitive threats.

Defining Family Enterprise

Throughout this book, the terms "family business," "family firm," and "family enterprise" are used interchangeably. However, each of these terms may also be used purposefully to identify a particular class of family-controlled and/or managed organization. When we refer to a *family business* or *family firm*, we are generally talking about an operating company of some type that is owned and/or operated by family members. This could be a manufacturing company, a professional services firm or retail business, for example. We strive to make this obvious to the reader through the context in which the term is used.

Families of wealth are also included in our definition of family enterprise. These stakeholders may have no direct involvement in any specific family-owned operating business, but they share (or expect to share) significant assets. These family stakeholders must make decisions together concerning their wealth, which may be held within complex structures and decision-making hierarchies that are prone to conflict, just as in a more conventional family business.

We use the term "family enterprise" to refer to the broader set of economic interests that are shared by family members. These economic interests may include a family business, a family-owned professional services firm, and may also include shared wealth, real estate, and other assets that are owned, managed or governed by family members. Family offices, organizations created by families to manage family wealth and/or philanthropy and to facilitate group decision-making, are also referred to as family enterprises. In addition, we sometimes refer to *"enterpris-*

ing families" – families who are purposefully connected by economic interests. Despite these differences, these terms may be used somewhat interchangeably throughout this book and *The Conflict Equation* methodology applies to all.

> A family enterprise is any organization in which important family relationships overlap with management, ownership or governance roles, and where these roles provide the family stakeholders with significant influence or control over that organization.

For the purpose of this book, we define a family enterprise as *any organization in which important family relationships overlap with management, ownership or governance roles, and where these roles provide the family stakeholders with significant influence or control over that organization.* In addition, the definition extends to organizations where such overlap may not currently exist, but *may be expected and planned for at some future time.* This may include sole proprietorships for which there are expectations of, and plans for, additional family member involvement in the future.

Families with Shared Wealth

Wealthy families who share assets grapple with many of the same challenges as families who share the ownership and management of a business. Like stakeholders in a more traditional operating company, these families need to manage their liquid and non-liquid assets and, therefore, need a level of structure to ensure they remain sustainable, continue to grow, and are used productively. To do this, wealthy families, like their business-owning counterparts, need strategies to manage the systemic conflict that comes from the intersection of their roles as family members, owners or beneficiaries, and stewards of their enterprise. To manage their assets and relationships over time, they must develop a shared vision, a communications structure, and guidelines by which they distribute funds. Philanthropy, a business in itself, often plays an important role in these families; carrying out shared philanthropy also requires a level of organizational rules and structure.

Family governance (how families make decisions together) provides a way for individual and groups of stakeholders to be proactive regarding their shared wealth. Privacy concerns, security, and education for beneficiaries all require planning. Additional needs such as risk management, tax and estate planning, and real estate management can be coordinated and overseen by a family office. As the level of complication and interdependence of stakeholders grows, so too does the potential for conflict.

Family Business

If you ask ten people to define "family business," you will probably get ten different answers. Some family business leaders aggressively promote the fact that they are family-owned and operated, believing that long-term family ownership implies quality and service commitments to customers and vendors. Other family business leaders are reluctant to identify their company as a "family" firm, believing that this term diminishes the value of their enterprise in the eyes of customers and competitors.

There is no SIC code (Standard Industrial Classification) or NAICS code (North American Industry Classification System) for family business. Family businesses are found across industrial sectors of all types. From family farms to high-tech manufacturing firms, and from retail stores to professional services firms, family businesses are ubiquitous. However, due to the fact that most family businesses are privately held companies, reliable data for family firms is far less available than for typical non-family businesses.

Family-run or family-controlled enterprises span all sizes and can be privately or publicly held. Fully one-third of the Fortune 500 businesses are family-managed and/or controlled. Family foundations and family offices are also included in our definition of family enterprise. They may have non-family executive management and only partial family ownership, yet may still be considered family-controlled.

Does Size Matter?

This book is intended primarily for situations where the family enterprise has some degree of complexity in its management, ownership and/or governance structure and where a multigenerational perspective exists. But, this book can also help families with smaller businesses and less complex ownership structures.

Smaller family enterprises may not make headlines when conflict strikes. But, while conflict in large family businesses can often seem sensational due to the huge dollar amounts involved, conflict in smaller companies, and within families of lesser means, can be just as, or more, extreme. This is because family stakeholders of larger companies may have more of an economic cushion than their smaller counterparts. Stakeholders of smaller family businesses are more likely to be faced with existential issues of basic economic survival when conflict strikes. In addition, a small business is far less able to withstand litigation. When these families argue, it can truly appear as a life-or-death struggle.

Family-run or controlled enterprises span all sizes and the value of these firms may not always correlate with the number of employees. Therefore, when we refer to a "large" or "small" family business, it is often useful to know if the company is large because it has many employees, possibly spread among several international offices, or because it has large revenues – or both. Some family foundations or family offices, which are also included in our definition of family enterprise, may have only a handful of employees yet manage and control very large and significant assets. In addition, some businesses may have very large revenues but may run on very slim margins and, thus, may have more in common with smaller businesses.

General contracting construction companies, for example, may have very large revenues but might actually be leaner firms with lower net incomes than one would expect. Likewise, real-estate-owning families may control great value through their properties, but may do so with relatively small staffs. Manufacturing firms, by contrast, are more likely to have significantly more people employed in their enterprise of equivalent value.

A family enterprise may have non-family, or "professional," leadership. It may even include non-family or other non-related families in its ownership group and on its board of directors. Public companies may also be considered family businesses, if a family holds a significant ownership stake such that it can extend significant strategic influence.

Defining Family

Throughout this book we refer to family relationships that are characterized as being permanent relationships – parent/child, siblings, and cousins, for example. Most often, these relationships are inherently important to the parties involved and there is a perception that breaking these ties would be catastrophic, with far-reaching effects on many of the other stakeholders involved. So, when we talk about "family," we are referring to individuals who typically share life-long relationships with each other, regardless of their personal affinity for each other.

Distant Family

Sometimes, late-generation family enterprises may be managed or owned by distant cousins. In these situations it is useful to ask, therefore, when does family stop being family? When do these distant family relationships cease to be significantly important relationships? When does calling the business a "family" business seem to lose its meaning – at least for the purposes of understanding and managing conflict?

The answer is different for each family. Some families have put in place structures such as family councils or family retreats that keep their family bonds meaningful despite distance and time. Other families quickly lose steam as "family." Even in these situations, when stakeholders no longer consider themselves "family," stakeholders may be locked into legacy agreements and structures that require them to act as "family." Therein also lie the seeds of conflict.

The term "family," therefore, is subjective and it is often difficult for outsiders to determine the importance of being family that really exists for family members. Sometimes, outsiders may perceive that a family member is acting against the business or against the family when they litigate or go to war in some manner. However, that family member may fervently believe that he or she is doing what is necessary to save both the business and the family. Stakeholders may end up in litigation against each other, when their real motivation is to save both themselves *and* the other from what they consider to be the other's misguided ideas. In other words, a family business in crisis may still be a family business, even when family stakeholders behave as enemies. As you'll see in later chapters, knowing when a family enterprise is "family" in name only is crucial for understanding how to approach the conflict management process and how to determine the likelihood of its success.

The Special Case of Spouses

One important distinction in the vast and diverse community of family enterprise concerns businesses owned and operated by married couples. When comparing such a leadership team to a team of siblings or first cousins that might lead a family business, for example, there is a similarity in that they are both single- (or same-) generation family businesses. What distinguishes the spousal team from the others, however, provides important insight into the concepts presented in this book.

When a married team leads a family business and conflict arises, there is an option not available to sibling- or cousin-led businesses. That option is divorce, which could render the enterprise a non-family-owned or managed business. For this reason, managing conflict when a married couple leads a firm often lends itself to more traditional approaches of dispute resolution. Siblings and cousins, however, remain family no matter what – even if cut off from each other due to conflict.

In addition, married couples typically do not have a lifetime of experience growing up together. In contrast, siblings and cousins experience each other as family in a far more permanent

> The importance of family relationships is a key component of family businesses and is what grounds our work in the conflict management framework we call *The Conflict Equation*.

way, typically beginning in childhood. For these reasons, family business conflicts involving siblings, cousins, parents-children and so on, often present extraordinary challenges that require an approach designed to address and preserve the integrity of these important family relationships.

That is not to say that spousal-led family businesses are of less concern. Spousal-led teams do indeed benefit from the robust approach to managing conflict we present in this book. Divorce is usually not the preferred conflict management choice, and improving the family bond is often a desired outcome. However, they represent a special case of family business because 1) they can choose to be non-family, through divorce, making the continuing relationship potentially less impactful, and 2) they haven't always been family, making certain aspects of the depth of their relationship potentially less impactful in the conflict management process.

The importance of family relationships is a key component of family businesses and is what grounds our work in the conflict management framework we call *The Conflict Equation*.

Importance of Continuing Relationships

A hallmark of family enterprise is that, on a fundamental level, the continuing relationships of the family members matter greatly. This poses both a challenge and benefit to managing conflict. The benefit is that family members should be able to leverage the importance of being family to better manage conflict. They may be more willing to compromise or to go the extra mile for a family member more than they would for non-family. However, too often family relationships become damaged during a conflict, rendering family members unable to achieve this advantage.

More commonly, however, being family is a complicating factor that makes managing conflict more difficult. This is because in addition to managing the substantive conflict issues at hand, the individuals are trying to negotiate how they will be family together during and after the conflict. Thus, the family relationships need to be considered at every stage of the conflict management process. This can be confusing and emotionally challenging for family members in conflict.

Contrast this with traditional civil disputes between non-family members. These combatants are concerned primarily about the substantive issues underlying the conflict and relationships issues do not matter nearly as much. This makes it a much simpler conflict landscape to navigate.

In family business conflict, the continuing family relationships are important – even when anger and distrust run high. Even when the individuals at the heart of the conflict feel that they don't care about their relationships any longer, they exist in a network of other family members who are affected by their conflict. Family members, although in conflict, will usually agree that breaking these ties would be devastating, with far-reaching effects on many other family members - even those only tangentially involved in a conflict.

Family relationships are lifelong. Even when family members abandon each other due to unresolved conflict and vow never to communicate again, the structural family bond still exists. You likely have experienced, or know someone who has experienced, a cutoff within his or her family. We frequently hear clients say "my sister and I never speak" or "my father and I had a falling out and only see each other, reluctantly, at infrequent family gatherings."

While cutoffs like these may curtail the active dispute that incited the original conflict, such a resolution generally is not a happy one for either party. Most importantly, despite the cutoff both the relationship and the systemic conflict still exist and continue to influence the family business system in some manner.

Certainly, non-family disputes can be extreme as well. But, non-related parties avoid the additional layer of complexity that exists in family conflict. In non-family disputes, once a resolution is reached, stakeholders can move on and may never have to hear about, let alone interact with, their adversary again. There generally is no sense of profound loss when ending casual friendships and business relationships as a result of a dispute, as there is with the destruction of a family relationship.

In addition, non-family relationships are not generally as intertwined with other relationships, the way family relationships tend to be. Unlike non-family relationships, disengaging from family relationships is often impossible or, at least, tremendously difficult, even when there is great animosity among family members, and becomes even more difficult when families are connected by economic interests because they need to continue to interact to manage those interests.

Another issue to note is that because of the highly emotional systems that exist in families, and the foundational importance that these relationships have played in stakeholders' lives, it is much more likely that the issues involved in a conflict speak to stakeholders' identities rather than simple disputes over money or any single event. We will discuss what we mean by identity-based conflict in more detail later in the book.

A Systems-Thinking Approach to Managing Family Business Conflict

Over more than a decade working with enterprising families, coupled with our own experience as stakeholders in our own family businesses, we identified consistent themes and components that existed in families that were either stuck or in active conflict. As we dove deeper into what was at play, we developed a methodology that became the foundation of our consulting practice, and it is the lens through which we look at a family business.

Our approach is grounded in *systems thinking*. Systems thinking is the process of thinking not simply about what is observed in isolation, but about how observed behavior is linked to other behaviors within a whole, integrated system. Nothing happens in a vacuum, and therefore all actions have ripple effects within the system. Accordingly, often what a group may think of as "the problem" may actually be the result of an array of issues that all came together over time to form a perfect storm.

Approaching conflict in a family business in the same manner as one would try to resolve a simple dispute among non-related stakeholders would not only be ineffective, but could even be counterproductive. Family business conflicts are systemic, not mere disputes, and therefore a systems approach that includes all stakeholders in their various roles and focuses on managing systemic conflict comprehensively is required. *Each dispute generally is part of a larger system, connected to, and influenced by, other disputes and relationship dynamics, which is why dispute resolution in general and mediation in particular are not effective processes for managing conflict over time in family business systems.*

> Our systems thinking approach begins by deconstructing family business conflict into each of the individual component parts that make up the conflict system.

To better understand why a systems approach to conflict management is so crucial, imagine a doctor treating a patient's cough without considering that person's medical history, changes in lifestyle or health, or other ailments. If a doctor did this, she might not fully understand the contributing factors to the condition and might therefore miss the opportunity to diagnose a more serious problem that, if caught early, could be treated and managed over the long term. By considering the patient's past and ongoing lifestyle, behavior and relationships, the doctor could gain valuable insight about whether the patient is able or likely to follow the prescribed protocol. Does the patient have the support he needs to follow doctor's orders? Is the patient surrounded by a peer group that encourages continued behavior that caused the illness or injury? This strategy of comprehensive assessment is akin to the systems methodology that we advocate using in working with families in conflict.

Accordingly, the following chapters offer families and their advisors ways to think beyond a current dispute; to understand the larger system behind the observed, individual events. We show how to consider the varied roles stakeholders play in order to understand their motivations and concerns and how those intersect with other stakeholders' motivations and concerns. We provide a method to assess the important continuing relationships that exist in the family business system, and how those relationships impact the causes of conflict and potential solutions to conflict.

Our systems thinking approach begins by deconstructing family business conflict into each of the individual component parts that make up the conflict system. These component parts are the various reasons, triggers, levers for improvement, and other characteristics that work together in the conflict system. Figuring out how these component parts interact to increase or decrease conflict is the goal of the systems approach to managing conflict. That goal is represented in *The Conflict Equation*.

The utility of *The Conflict Equation* is that it establishes a method that considers the causes of conflict impacting the entire family business system, while also leading the stakeholder in a family enterprise (or an advisor to these families) to solutions that are robust, reliable, and transformational.

In the following chapters you will learn how to deconstruct what is going on in the family business system and how to generate approaches that will help manage existing and future conflict, as well as repair damage done in the past.

Summary
- We use the term "family enterprise" to refer to families who either share wealth or who share ownership and management of an operating company. Often, the management of a family's wealth is done through an operating company (i.e., a family office).
- The importance of continuing relationships must be considered throughout the conflict management process.
- Understanding how to manage conflict in a family business is important because family businesses are so prevalent and critical to our economy, and because conflict is built into the family business system. The ability of family members to be effective contributors to their shared enterprise, and for that enterprise to be of true benefit to the family, is fraught with potential for conflict. Only through understanding the unique qualities that define

this type of conflict, and learning to manage them, can success in family business be a potential outcome.

- Family business conflicts are so extreme because they are not simple disagreements over substantive issues like money or employment. These conflicts are more often rooted in identity issues among stakeholders. There is so much at stake with a role in the family business, or access to family wealth, that it is fundamentally unlike the situation in a non-family firm. Roles in a family business are often self-defining for stakeholders, i.e., the difference between perceived success or failure in their lives.

- These conflicts are so difficult to manage because the conflicts themselves are systemic, rather than simple disputes about isolated events. They are also so intractable due to the importance of the continuing family relationships that must be considered at every stage of the conflict management process. Ongoing family relationships are an extraordinarily complicating factor. Stakeholders are not only trying to manage the substance of the conflict at hand, they are also trying to figure out how they will be "family" in the future.

- When approaching your own, or a client's, family business conflict, the biggest mistake is to underestimate the complexity of conflict in family business.

Chapter 2

Understanding Conflict in a Family Enterprise

All treaties between great states cease to be binding when they come in conflict with the struggle for existence.

— Otto von Bismarck

The focus of this book is on understanding and managing conflict – not eliminating it. Why? Conflict plays a very valuable role in human endeavor. It is only through being challenged by conflict that we learn, grow, and advance as individuals, families, companies, and societies. Well-managed conflict can lead to new approaches, innovative strategies, and resilience. It can lead to useful ideas about sharing power, mutual respect, productive conversation, and good planning. It is absolutely possible for families to learn to manage family business conflict in constructive ways that ensure the success of their families and their businesses for generations to come.

> Learning how to properly manage conflict is a unique and powerful competitive advantage for families and their enterprises.

Conversely, attempting to avoid or ignore conflict can lead to stagnating relationships and organizations. Not dealing with conflict leads to the slow erosion of relationships, the development of grudges and counterproductive behaviors, and can cause stakeholders and their organizations (both family and business) to miss valuable opportunities.

Even more concerning is that improperly managing conflict can lead to increased conflict and waste valuable resources such as time, money, human capital, and reputation. Learning how to properly manage conflict, therefore, is a unique and powerful competitive advantage for families and their enterprises.

Because conflict is built into the structure of a family business, the methodology described in this book takes a comprehensive approach and deals with conflict systemically, in a manner designed to support important continuing family relationships. In our experience, this is the only approach that has the possibility of a lasting and resilient outcome. We believe that managing conflict in a family business requires a logical organizing structure for the application of a wide variety of skill sets to *manage, not resolve*, systemic conflict, and to preserve and strengthen family relationships.

> Managing conflict in a family business requires a logical organizing structure for the application of a wide variety of skill sets to *manage, not resolve*, systemic conflict and to preserve and strengthen family relationships.

Emotions run high in families and these emotions are amplified when families find themselves in conflict over business, wealth, and power. Expectations of love and support, the need for acknowledgment, and complex family histories magnify reactions to what might be normal disagreements between non-family members in non-family enterprises. Business decisions, good or bad, are often perceived by family stakeholders as indicators of family affinity, and this may have a particularly strong impact on individuals raised in an enterprising family.

For any conflict management methodology to be effective for family businesses, dealing with emotion, relationships, and psychological issues must be fully integrated with how that methodology addresses the substantive issues of money and power that often seem to be the presenting problems. Accordingly, any methodology that attempts to manage conflict in a family business must not marginalize or set aside the strong emotions involved. The beauty of *The Conflict Equation* is that it allows users to understand and address all components of conflict **simultaneously**.

Throughout this book, we are not only addressing how to manage active conflict that is easily identifiable when it arises, but also how to manage the more subtle or passive conflict that often exists in family enterprise. Passive conflict is insidious; it lurks beneath the surface and causes great damage when stakeholders look the other way. It is what gets stakeholders stuck, unable to make good decisions in a timely manner. Often, passive conflict arises because stakeholders fear the active conflict that will result from making those decisions. It is what causes stakeholders to stop sharing information, to silo in their organizations and to exclude one another from having influence on their organization. Or, in the most extreme cases, passive conflict is what causes stakeholders to block or sabotage another family member's efforts. In this chapter, we dig deeper into how we understand conflict in family enterprise.

> Passive conflict is insidious; it lurks beneath the surface and causes great damage when stakeholders look the other way. It gets stakeholders stuck.

Why Does Conflict Occur?

From the moment we are born, we are engaged in an endless struggle to satisfy our needs. As individuals, our real and perceived needs develop differently over time, and we each develop different skills and levels of ability in satisfying those needs. It is a messy process with false starts, failed attempts, regrets and, occasionally, brilliant successes.

Conflict develops when someone, or some group, seeking to satisfy his or her own needs, interferes unjustly (in our opinion) with our own search for needs satisfaction. Often, parties are completely unaware of the threat they pose to another's attempts at needs fulfillment. Nor are they always aware of how essential the fulfillment of a particular need might be to another's basic survival or life purpose. These struggles can fester for ages, and even take on a life of their own, with nobody really understanding why the conflict even started in the first place. Passive, unintended conflicts can continue as family "traditions" even after the originators are long gone.

Rarely does conflict occur because of one person's sociopathic desire to simply deprive another person of their needs. Although individuals whose core needs are met through the pain and suffering of others are rare, revenge is not an uncommon motivation and is quite different from taking pleasure in the pain of others. Revenge is intended to serve a practical end – to teach a lesson that will make an undesired outcome less likely in the future, or to elicit (or force) an offer of settlement.

The work of psychologist Abraham Maslow is particularly helpful when thinking about identity-based conflict. Maslow believed that individuals all struggle to create meaning as they strive to meet their basic needs, which become increasingly sophisticated as they succeed at each level and move on to the next. In Maslow's vision, humans all strive to meet ever-increasing needs as they move through life. Conflict occurs when individuals (and groups) are unable to satisfy these needs due to the perceived interference of others.

Figure 2-1 is an illustration of Maslow's "Hierarchy of Needs." The hierarchy begins at the bottom with the most basic needs like food, water and shelter, and moves steadily to more-sophisticated pursuits. It's as simple as once you're fed, you'd like a shelter to sleep in, and once you have that, you'd like to sleep without fear of being attacked, and once you have that, you'd like some friends, and so on. Maslow believed that we have general needs that must be met in order for us to behave unselfishly and lead meaningful lives.

At the top of Maslow's hierarchy is something he calls "self-actualization." Self-actualization occurs when individuals feel that they have achieved all their subordinate needs and now have the opportunity and resources to truly achieve their ultimate potential as human beings.

Figure 2-1   *Maslow's Hierarchy of Needs Pyramid*

We can use Maslow's hierarchy as an analogy for family business stakeholders. For example, access to basic employment, salary and/or dividends might produce the resources needed to satisfy basic physiological needs for some stakeholders. Keep in mind that physiological needs are relative to what a person was accustomed to in their formative years, or to the peer group with whom they have come to identify. What might be considered a luxury to one person may be perceived as a very real need by another.

Ownership, a role in management, or some degree of power and control might serve someone's need to feel safe and secure. Family employees may have put all their eggs in the family business basket and may not have developed the transferrable skills needed to succeed outside the family company. When their employment at the family firm is threatened, it may seem like an existential threat to their basic survival.

Having an office to go to, colleagues to interact with, and vendors and customers who depend on you all satisfy a strong need for belonging and acceptance that serves social needs. In addition, access to family wealth may provide entry into the only social world that a person has identified with for decades and which defines who they are. The sense of belonging that a role in the family business, or even a token share of stock, brings might be important in satisfying a social need that neither money nor a job at another firm could match.

An important title, a seat on the board, an expensive car, the ability to fly first class, or access to the company jet might serve esteem needs. Having the authority that goes along with a certain status in an organization, or the respect that comes from being a proven leader at the family business, also serves esteem needs.

Self-actualization is an inherent need of most people. It is what drives us to excel. The ability to achieve one's potential, to have ample resources to do so, and not to have to ask anyone for permission, is a fantasy for most people. But family business leaders, to a large extent, are able to control their own destiny. The ability to innovate and create – and to shoulder great responsibility – is what drives most entrepreneurs. It is their drive to self-actualize that lies at the heart of their success as leaders.

It is critical to note that Maslow's hierarchy focuses on the satisfaction of *needs*. In our framework, *The Conflict Equation*, we deconstruct Maslow's idea of *needs* into two component parts: values and goals. Our individual goals are driven by the values we have developed over our lifetimes. These goals are chosen to satisfy our perceived needs. Even our most basic survival needs, therefore, are influenced by the value systems we come from. Survival, the need for food and shelter, may mean something very different to someone raised with affluence than to someone raised in poverty.

Identity-Based Conflict

When any individual or group gets in the way of our attempts to satisfy the needs we identify as core to our purpose in life, conflict of the most extreme type – identity-based conflict – can occur.

Values and Personality

We are not defined solely by our needs, however. We have values that go beyond simply driving our goals. Our values are a big part of our individual identities. We define ourselves by our political and religious affiliations, for example. These affiliations reflect our deeply held values. We define ourselves by our moral principles, by the cars we drive, how we raise our children, and where we go on vacation. So much of who we are is driven by the unique complement of values we hold.

We each have unique personalities, inherent skills and interests that mesh with our values and our goals. We are outgoing, introverted, artistic, smart, funny, risk-averse, entrepreneurial, carefree, or an endless combination of qualities and characteristics that define us. We like to read, play music or participate in sports. Some of us are talented; some are smarter than others. We each have hobbies and unique sexual identities. Some of us are athletic and some of us are less physically able.

> When we feel that our identity is not acknowledged and accepted, we feel unsafe and our fight-or-flight-or-freeze response is triggered, rendering us unable to deal with that person or group rationally.

Conflict can develop when an individual's values or personality clash with another's. When an individual rejects our values or personalities as antithetical to theirs, a very important thing happens. When we feel that our identity is not acknowledged and accepted by someone with whom we are engaged in some manner, we feel unsafe and our fight-flight-or-freeze response is triggered, rendering us unable to deal with that person or group rationally. This is the case even when there is a misunderstanding and one only perceives that their identity is not understood or accepted by another. Any approach for managing conflict, therefore, must address these highly emotional factors as well.

This same analysis can be applied to groups. While groups do not have personalities per se, they have histories, values-driven goals, ways of getting things done, belief systems, spokesmen, policies and a host of defining group qualities. Groups, just like individuals, can get into identity-based conflicts with both individuals and other groups.

In a family business, these groups may be identified as family branches, different generations, those who attended one college versus another, those who have more money than others, in-laws, those employed in the business, owners versus non-owners, or a host of other categorizations. Each group may represent different values, different interests or goals, and have a unique way of communicating – just like individuals.

Roles

Finally, we each play specific roles in our lives. Some of those roles we were born into and did not choose: Son, Daughter, Cousin, Family Business or Wealth Stakeholder. Some roles we have chosen: Husband, Wife, Parent, Stepparent, Family Business Manager. The important thing about roles is that they are meaningful only in regard to their relationship with others. One cannot be a parent without a child. One cannot be a manager in a family business without a family business.

Sometimes, these roles are merely situational and only of limited importance to stakeholders' lives. A role in the family business may simply be a job that for some stakeholders could easily be replaced. For others, a role in the family enterprise may strike to the heart of that stakeholder's identity. In many cases, stakeholders have devoted their lives to their family enterprise. They may have earned their degrees and made the sacrifices expected of them in pursuit of the future they believe they were promised, or are entitled to, in the family enterprise. Stakeholders may have identified with a role in the family business from childhood; and giving up childhood dreams is not easy. For family business stakeholders, therefore, it is often not simply about a "job" or "shares" or "money" – it is often about identity. Since an individual's identity is not something that can be negotiated, so too will it be unlikely that a stakeholder's role in the family enterprise would be up for negotiation when conflict breaks out.

Some stakeholders may have relied upon the family enterprise for lifetime support and may be ill-equipped to make it on their own without a role in the business, or a share of the family wealth. These stakeholders may see their role in the family enterprise as essential for basic survival, or at least for the maintenance of the only lifestyle they believe they are equipped to handle. Entitlement as a birthright, nurtured by a privileged upbringing, is a powerful force to contend with when conflict develops. Like identity, survival is equally non-negotiable.

Outsiders to family business may not fully understand the existential threat that stakeholders feel when their role in a family business is threatened. Even when stakeholders feel trapped in a role they don't want, they may see few alternatives. When family members have devoted the bulk of their career to their family's business, for example, they often believe that they have limited options outside of the family business. Outside firms may be suspicious of the experience that someone has had at their own family's business. An outside employer might anticipate that the family employee may not have had appropriate accountability standards due to his or her last name. The outside employer may just feel that the family employee wouldn't fit into a "real" company hierarchy. Family employees may feel desperate at the thought of drastic change to their role in the family enterprise: a role that they may feel entitled to or promised.

Make no mistake; this is often not just an emotional crisis. These stakeholders are fighting for security on some of the most basic levels of their version of the "needs pyramid": food, shelter and safety. As a result, if their struggles are not handled properly, the battles can become very heated indeed. Even the mildest attempts to examine or renegotiate roles, policies, and money may be perceived as an attack on a stakeholder's fundamental identity and security, further polarizing stakeholders and exacerbating conflict.

Whatever the underlying reason — promises relied upon, sacrifices made, expectations encouraged, feelings of entitlement, outright need — stakeholder roles in a family enterprise are less negotiable than they might otherwise be in a non-family enterprise. To some stakeholders in a family enterprise, the roles they play reflect their perception of who they are in the world, and negotiating one's identity is not possible.

Moreover, concern about stakeholders' identities is the hidden subtext of negotiations and discussions at every stage of both the conflict and the conflict management process. In addition to trying to negotiate solutions to specific disputes, families in this type of identity-based, systemic conflict are

> Identity is not negotiable.

also trying to define what their continued role (i.e., identity) will be in the *family* post-conflict. How combatants, and other family members impacted by conflict, will continue to "be family" in the future is a fundamental issue that is rarely discussed during a dispute resolution process.

Conflict vs. Dispute

It is important to distinguish between what is a dispute and what is a conflict. While at first blush this distinction may seem merely semantic, it is actually profound. A dispute is an isolated issue on which two people or factions disagree. The disagreement may be about money, a promise made and not kept, or something trivial like what movie to see. While it may often be difficult, a dispute can usually be resolved with a decision in one party's favor or with a compromise of sorts. There is an entire industry set up to help stakeholders resolve disputes, as well as a robust body of knowledge and technique for doing so.

Because family business stakeholders have such interdependent relationships, it is likely that the issues they are grappling with are not merely isolated disputes. Since they are connected by family relationship, as well as ownership and management structures, it is more likely that they are dealing with conflicts that are systemic in nature – involving issues that transcend any single role they play.

A conflict is not an isolated issue. Rather, it is a controversy within a larger series of moving parts where stakeholders' roles overlap and where there may be significantly more than only two disputants. Although a conflict may appear to be a series of interrelated disputes, if its management is approached dispute by dispute, whack-a-mole style, such a conflict, especially one in a family business, can quickly escalate.

One reason for this escalation is that if a conflict – over a salary, for example – is treated as a simple dispute, it is likely that the majority of effort would be expended in arguing and focusing on the economic dispute at hand. The underlying, and typically unarticulated, relationship issues will flounder or proceed chaotically. Often, in a family business, the relationship issues turn out to be more important factors than the presenting economic "dispute." Yet, these non-economic issues often get overlooked in the rush to deal with the more tangible issues at hand — such as a raise, a business or investment strategy, a bonus, ownership or control.

Another reason trying to approach a conflict as a series of individual disputes often makes matters worse is that dispute resolution cannot take into account how each individual dispute is connected to each other dispute or how the fabric of relationships and histories intersect and co-exist. In systemic conflict, resolving one dispute may simply serve to make others worse. It is in the connections among individual disputes that conflict is defined. Only by understanding these connections can one hope to manage a conflict successfully.

For example, resolving a dispute about the salary for a son in the family business may bring up fairness issues with other children in the business, causing additional, and perhaps more complicated, problems.

What connects these disputes may be more important than any individual dispute. A father and son in a seemingly endless battle over roles in the family business may have been advised that "they just can't work together" and that one of them must leave. However, roles in a family business are so intertwined with family relationships that separation from the business may threaten the family relationship itself. A role in the family enterprise may represent, for one or both stakeholders, the glue that bonds family members together. The role in the family business may be perceived as evidence of love, respect, acknowledgement, or trust. A failure to find solutions to a family business conflict may, therefore, serve to negate or irreparably damage the family bond.

Paradoxically, keeping a family business conflict alive may actually be the only way that stakeholders believe their relationship can be kept alive. A conflictual relationship may be perceived as better than no relationship at all. This begs the question which is often at play in some family businesses: how do you help manage a conflict when the stakeholders are more invested in keeping the battle going than in achieving resolution?

The answer to this question is that focusing on resolutions to individual disputes is clearly insufficient and potentially destructive. A comprehensive approach to managing conflict that deals with conflict systemically, and which is designed to support important continuing relationships, is the only approach that has the possibility of a lasting and resilient outcome in family enterprise systems.

Does this sound like a tall order? After all, businesses and families are complicated. Their combination is exponentially more complicated. Substantive disputes might require expertise in accounting, law, finance, or business operations and strategy. Family issues might require expertise in family systems, individual and family therapy, substance abuse counseling, and family mediation. Ownership issues may require expertise in estate planning, valuation, and investment strategy. These conflicts are complex and they do not respond to short cuts or simple solutions. A complex and collaborative set of skills must be applied in proper sequence for successful management of this type of systemic conflict.

It is precisely because of this unavoidable complexity in managing family business conflict that we developed *The Conflict Equation*. It helps manage this complexity by deconstructing conflict into its component parts, showing how these parts fit together in the conflict system, and providing a roadmap for developing approaches to managing all aspects of a conflict.

Interdependence

Whether we are looking at conflict among individuals or groups, one thing is clear: Conflict can exist only when individuals and groups are interdependent in some manner. This interdependence may be purposeful or simply unavoidable. Conflict in a family business is particularly common because there are so many levels of interdependence built into its structure. This will become clearer as we explore the structure of family enterprise and learn about all the overlapping systems and interdependent roles that make up the family enterprise in Chapter 9.

It is intuitively obvious that when individuals or groups are completely unconnected, and there is zero interdependence between or among them, conflict simply cannot exist. The more interdependent individuals and groups are with each other, the more opportunity there is for conflict to develop. It is hard to imagine a more interdependent group of stakeholders than those who are members of an enterprising family or who are involved in a family business.

Interdependence can also be subjective and it is the perception of interdependence that truly drives conflict. Expectations run high in enterprising families. This is especially true when estate and succession plans are unclear or not discussed. When individuals and groups behave according to their expectations, they are doing so based on perceived or expected interdependence in the future. Whether interdependence is real or perceived, it still matters. William Wilmot and Joyce Hocker, in their textbook *Interpersonal Conflict*, highlighted the interdependence of parties as a major factor affecting their level of conflict. Because interdependence is a fundamental condition for conflict to exist, and family enterprise is rife with interdependent relationships, the potential for conflict is built into the family business system.

> Conflict can exist only when individuals and groups are interdependent in some manner.

External Factors

Sometimes families find themselves in conflict through no fault or failure of their own. Economies falter, vendors prove unreliable, competitive threats sometimes come out of nowhere, and illness and death can occur without notice. These are external stressors on any organization.

It is useful to always have contingency plans and to always be prepared for anything, but prescience is impossible and, sometimes, external factors have an impact on the success or failure of a family enterprise. It is important for families to understand when conflict is situational, coming from outside their family business system, and when it comes from the dynamics at play within their system.

Economic cycles, changing market dynamics, regulatory issues, technology advances and other external factors can raise the level of stress in a family business system, making stakeholders more reactive and sensitive to conflict. *The Conflict Equation* considers these external sources of conflict as well, and alerts stakeholders to be vigilant in preparing for the unexpected.

Time

The importance of time is fundamental to our thinking about conflict management and cannot be underestimated. It takes time for relationships to form, opinions to harden, conflicts to fester. Families do not wake up to intractable conflict overnight. Time colors our perceptions of the past and it takes time for any remedy for a conflict to take root and impact relationships for the future.

Individual family stakeholders see only a snapshot in time of any situation, and advisors see even less. Both must recognize that it took a long time for a family to get where it is now and it will take time for the family to move forward. Everyone knows that change is difficult, and factoring in the impact of time on conflict management is crucial.

Even the most well-intentioned and carefully thought out conflict management approach might initially increase conflict as it may require difficult conversations and may forge new, initially uncomfortable, relationships among stakeholders. Understanding and anticipating these time lags and the fact that things may get worse before they get better, is a crucial insight required of anyone who attempts to manage conflict in a family enterprise.

When stakeholders have appropriate expectations regarding the conflict management work needed and the impact and timing of the various conflict management approaches they have embarked on, they can weather these transitions better and stay the course to ultimately lower the level of conflict in their relationships and their enterprise. *The Conflict Equation* calls attention to the impact of time on all aspects of the conflict situation.

The Conflict Equation

The Conflict Equation identifies twelve components of conflict and combines them into a qualitative mathematical formula. Its purpose is not to determine a numerical value for conflict or to gauge any of its components on some type of number line. Rather, the equation format is only used to show the logical relationship among all twelve components of conflict and how each influences every other and the overall level of conflict in the family enterprise system. In this way, it is a powerful tool for understanding and managing conflict. When seemingly intractable, unfathomable conflicts among family members occur, as they often do when family work or own together, deconstructing these conflicts into their component parts and understanding how each component part contributes to the quagmire enables stakeholders to be purposeful in managing their own behavior and decision-making so that conflict can be managed.

If there are deficiencies and weaknesses in the firm that no stakeholder has identified, and these are not causing conflict, this process may not identify them and they can remain unaddressed. *The Conflict Equation* process is not intended as a method for general business consulting and it cannot replace the value of industry experts for assessing business operations. *The Conflict Equation* process is only intended to identify what is blocking stakeholders from achieving their interests and inhibiting organizations from moving forward, while also laying out options to help move the system forward.

The Conflict Equation identifies and helps clear away whatever is blocking all stakeholders from achieving their potential and offers a path forward. It includes the use of several targeted tools, initiates strategic discussions on a wide variety of topics that helps stakeholders identify gaps in knowledge and skills, and lays out a roadmap for bringing in the additional strategic resources needed to supplement stakeholders' knowledge and skill sets. It is surprising how often breakthroughs in managing conflict from deconstructing it with *The Conflict Equation* approach yield significant bottom line improvements to a family business.

Summary

- Identity-based conflict is not negotiable.
- Conflict occurs for many reasons, all of which are interrelated.
- There is a major distinction between dispute resolution and conflict management.
- The greater the level of interdependence of stakeholders, the greater the potential for conflict.
- Factors outside the control of family members, external factors, can influence the level of conflict in a family business system.
- The element of time must be considered when evaluating the level of or potential for conflict in a family business

system or approaches to managing it. Family enterprises develop over time. *The Conflict Equation* provides a snapshot in time. Conflict management approaches take time to create change.

- The methodology of *The Conflict Equation* doesn't provide specific answers; it provides a roadmap that illustrates why a family enterprise is stuck or in conflict and what approaches are needed to move the system forward. Answers evolve naturally from stakeholders when properly guided by *The Conflict Equation*.

Chapter 3

Deconstructing the Conflict System

Do not worry about your difficulties in Mathematics. I can assure you mine are still greater.
— Albert Einstein

The Conflict Equation was not designed as a quick fix. Rather, it was developed to provide a logical, organizing structure to manage, not resolve, systemic conflict in family enterprise. Its ultimate goal is to help family business stakeholders get "unstuck" by understanding where conflict in a family business system is coming from in order to make the business stronger and more sustainable while preserving and strengthening family relationships. It provides a roadmap for stakeholders and their advisors to properly engage with the family business system to manage conflict effectively when continuing relationships matter.

Any systems approach to understanding conflict in a family business system must contain all the components involved in the conflict system. These components must then be represented in a manner that shows how each component interacts with other components to increase or decrease conflict.

In this chapter, we introduce the general components of "identity-based conflict when continuing relationships matter" – i.e., conflict in a family enterprise – and describe how each component serves to increase or reduce conflict and how it acts on each of the other components. In this way, we will build *The Conflict Equation*. Subsequent chapters will drill down into each detailed component as *The Conflict Equation* is built.

The Power of the Equation Format

Once any system is understood sufficiently, it is often possible to apply mathematical modeling to offer a clearer understanding of how the system has worked historically, to provide some degree of predictability for how the system will function in the future, and how it will react to new situations when changes are made to any of its components.

We developed *The Conflict Equation* by applying systems thinking processes to family businesses that are rife with identity-based, systemic conflict, where continuing relationships matter. It is important to understand that **human behavior cannot be reduced to numbers and *The Conflict Equation* is not intended to be quantitative.** We do not plug in numbers, so there will not be a numerical answer to the equation or actual calculations to make.

Rather, *The Conflict Equation* is a qualitative formula identifying each of the key components of conflict in a family business system, and how these elements interact to increase or decrease the level of conflict in the family business system. The advantage of defining a system mathematically in this way is that a mathematical equation can present individual components and their interrelationships *simultaneously*. This allows users to see the effect on the whole system when one component (economic or emotional) or another changes.

> Think of *The Conflict Equation* as algebraic shorthand to help you keep track of all the components of conflict involved. The advantage of defining a system mathematically is that a mathematical equation can present individual factors and relationships *simultaneously*.

Think of *The Conflict Equation* as algebraic shorthand to help you keep track of all the components involved in conflict of this type. Having such a tool ensures that nothing is missed and that each component is understood in relation to each other component. If you find equations daunting, think of *The Conflict Equation* as an organized checklist that will help you identify and clarify all the elements of conflict in a given situation, and help you think through all the different approaches you can apply to manage that conflict.

Everyday Equations

We intuitively think in equations, though we may not always be aware of it. When we think about how long it will take to get to a friend's house in another town, we think about traffic on the highway and the speed limit of various routes. Our minds do a qualitative calculation and let us know, based on available information, when we need to leave in order to arrive on time.

We even consider complex variables like the time it would take to get gas or stop off to buy a gift. And, we consider the unexpected – the flat tire, the fender bender, and the possibility of getting a ticket. Our minds calculate the probability of all these events automatically and weight the time each would take against the other factors.

One might consider taking the time to write out all these factors in an algebraic equation, but there would not be much sense in doing so. The consequences of getting to the friend's house a few minutes later or earlier are fairly insignificant. So our gut feeling, informed by our mind's informal calculating ability, is sufficient.

What if we were figuring out how to get to the moon? NASA had this very challenge and knew it was important to map out every contingency they could think of. With so much at stake, leaving it to "gut feel" was not an option. Not that managing a family business is analogous to a flight to the moon, but there is a lot at stake when conflict threatens an enterprising family. So, pursuing conflict management strategies based on gut feel, for a family business, seems irresponsible and foolhardy.

Fortunately, *The Conflict Equation* provides a middle ground. It is both possible and extremely useful to craft non-numerical equations that reveal what is going on in these complex situations. While doing so may not provide an "answer," it can guide a process. *The Conflict Equation* is such an equation. It captures the components that are involved in understanding and managing conflict and shows how these components are interrelated. Examining conflict through the lens of *The Conflict Equation* ensures that the conflict advisor and stakeholders do not miss anything, and that all avenues of conflict management are explored.

A Preview of *The Conflict Equation*

In order to give readers some perspective about where we are headed, the general, or simplified, form of the equation is presented below:

$$\text{Conflict*} \propto \frac{\text{Interdependence x Trigger x Reasons}}{\text{Family Factor x Conflict Management Approaches}} + \text{External Factors}$$

Key
* Where conflict is considered over the course of time
$\propto$ is the mathematical symbol for "proportional to"

Figure 3-1

This general form of the equation shows that there are seven categories of conflict components that we need to identify and learn about. These are:

- Time for conflict to develop and respond to management,
- Reasons for conflict,
- the Trigger for conflict,
- the Family Factor ™,
- Conflict Management Approaches,
- Interdependence, and
- External factors.

In the following chapters, we will deconstruct all the components of conflict in detail, building it back up into its complete form that includes twelve individual components that define conflict in a family business and provides a roadmap for its management.

We have already learned about our first component of conflict, Interdependence, in Chapter 2. Conflict cannot exist without some degree of interdependence. In Chapter 9, we will describe how to evaluate the level of interdependence in the particular family business system being considered. For now, however, we will begin building our equation with this single concept category. We are starting simply, with only one conflict component, in order to show how the equation format works.

We know that the more interdependent stakeholders are, the more the potential for conflict exists. It is clear that if two people are in completely separate places with no communication, shared assets or overlapping roles, they cannot experience conflict with each other. Accordingly, we know that if there is zero Interdependence, there can be zero conflict. An algebraic expression that conveys this relationship is:

Conflict is proportional to Interdependence

Or, as abbreviated:

$$C \propto ID$$

Key
C = Conflict $\propto$ = is proportional to   ID = Interdependence

Figure 3-2

In Figure 3-2, C is the level of conflict, ID is the level of interdependence, and $\propto$ is the algebraic expression "proportional to."

We use the term "proportional to" in order to indicate that we are interested in relationships among components, *not* in specific quantities or numbers.

While this simple equation is not a complete description of conflict in a family business, it is a start. It tells us that if we want to reduce conflict, we might consider reducing interdependence – and this makes sense. However, this overly simplistic model would lead us to the conclusion that the only way to reduce conflict in a family business is to separate business from family, and to separate individuals from each other as much as possible. This thinking would lead to siloing in the workplace, selling the family business, and eliminating family leadership succession plans, thereby ceasing all of the family's conflictual (and productive) connections.

Such thinking may seem antithetical to anyone in a family business, but it is surprising how many advisors actually believe that the best family businesses are ones where the family has been removed from the business! Advisors who believe this are operating under the overly simplistic paradigm shown above — looking for simple answers to the complex problems of complex systems. Fortunately, the conflict system in family business is more complex than this and it provides many opportunities for successful outcomes when all the conflict components are considered.

As we deconstruct family business conflict into more component parts, we will describe how each part impacts the conflict system and we will expand the equation so that each additional component is incorporated in a way that makes sense algebraically to describe how that component actually impacts the conflict system. To that end, we will build a complete representation of the family business conflict system in an equation format.

How It Works

Conflict is an indication that something is not functioning correctly in the family business system. Just as a fever indicates that there is something wrong with an individual's health, conflict tells us that we need to take a deeper look into what is going on in a system of human interaction. How serious is the illness? What experts do we need? Properly understood and managed, conflict can serve a very important function in family business – it is the immune system for the family enterprise.

Think of *The Conflict Equation* like the dashboard in a car. Things can go wrong in a car – indicator lights will flash, gauges will show when fuel is low or washer fluid is needed. The instrument panel also identifies the information needed to drive safely. It tells you how fast you're going, and many cars now warn you of an impending crash or if you're drifting out of your lane. In a similar manner, *The Conflict Equation* not only indicates the level of conflict in the system, but by identifying each of the individual components of conflict, it also gives users the ability to improve the functioning of the family enterprise. Think of *The Conflict Equation* as a dashboard, not for corporate performance, but for managing conflict in the family enterprise, and thus, its health.

To fully appreciate the power of *The Conflict Equation*, a basic understanding of fractions, addition and multiplication is required. Don't worry – no actual calculations are required and the math we present is very simple.

Think of a fraction. A fraction is composed of a numerator on top and a denominator on the bottom. If the numerator is large and the denominator is small, like 100/2, the result is a large number (i.e., 50 – larger than the denominator). When the numerator is small and the denominator is large, like 2/100, the result is a small number (i.e., 0.02 – smaller than the denominator). When the numerator is 0, like 0/10, the result is zero. And, when the denominator is zero – well, here we have a small problem.

As the denominator of a fraction approaches zero, the actual result of the fraction gets progressively larger and approaches infinity. But, mathematicians have a rule – the denominator can never actually be zero or the fraction loses all meaning. This can be difficult to comprehend. To explain it, think about a plate of 10 cookies to be shared. If there are 10 people, each gets one, if there are 5 people, each gets 2, if there are 3 people, each gets 3 1/3. But if there are no people, nothing happens – the cookies don't get shared. There's no answer because the concept of sharing the cookies is meaningless when there are zero people in the equation. As you will see, we have crafted *The Conflict Equation* to deal with this complication elegantly. In *The Conflict Equation*, the denominator can be very small, but never actually zero.

How is *The Conflict Equation* Helpful?

The equation is helpful because it simultaneously shows the relationship between a particular family's reasons for conflict, what triggers active conflict and what leverage exists to lower the overall level of systemic conflict.

For our purposes, and we will explain this later in greater detail, a large numerator and small denominator indicate a high degree of conflict in the system. If we can do something to make the numerator smaller and the denominator bigger, conflict will lessen. Either way, the equation will tell us what is going on, why conflict exists and what can be done about it. It is up to the stakeholders to choose the solutions laid bare by the equation – or not.

The only other mathematical concept you need beyond understanding fractions is an understanding of how parentheses are used in an equation (what is also called "order of operations"). For example: $2 \times (2 + 4 + 3)$ is the same as 2×9, or 18. The order of the terms within the parentheses does not matter. We could write the equation as $2 \times (3 + 2 + 4)$ and we will still get the same answer, 18. If the numbers inside the parentheses were changed, but still added up to 9, the answer would be the same.

$$2 \times (2 + 4 + 3)$$
is the same as
$$2 \times (5 + 1 + 3)$$
and is the same as
$$2 \times 9$$
Each formula, therefore, equals 18

Figure 3-3

A common shorthand used with parentheses in an equation is to omit the "x" that stands for multiplication. When a number precedes a function in parentheses without any mathematical sign, multiplication is assumed. Therefore, the two equations shown in Figure 3-4 provide the same result.

$$2 \times (2 + 4 + 3) \text{ is the same as } 2 (2 + 4 + 3)$$

Figure 3-4

Finally, and most importantly, we will not be using numbers. Instead, we will be using words. This will become clear as we develop the equation together in the coming chapters.

Component Categories of *The Conflict Equation*

In the coming chapters, we will build *The Conflict Equation* in detail as we fully deconstruct conflict into its component parts. For now, it is useful to present the equation in a very general, or simplified, form using some of the components already discussed and general categories for terms yet to be described.

We already discussed the first term, Interdependence, and we learned how it impacts a very simple system of conflict. In Chapter 2, we were also introduced to two additional components: External Factors and Time.

As can be seen from the general form of the equation shown in Figure 3-5, External Factors are simply added to a more complicated part of the equation. This tells us that sometimes conflict arises outside of the system under stakeholder control.

Time is included as a subscript of Conflict itself. It serves only to remind us that Time needs to be considered, but it does not have a specific mathematical function. It is only included in the equation as a reminder that conflict took time to develop and that each component behaves differently with time. Some components react quickly and some take more time to develop. When we evaluate conflict we are looking only at a point in time. Any ideas we generate for managing conflict will take time to have an effect on the overall level of conflict. Adding Time to the equation tells us to take a step back to consider the past, present and future, and to have patience with this process.

Reasons for Conflict – Chapter 4 is devoted to the identification and understanding of the three Reasons that underlie all conflict. When the reasons that underlie conflict are articulated and understood, there will be clarity on exactly why a family and their organization gets stuck, unable to move forward and make important decisions in a timely manner.

Trigger for Conflict – Chapter 5 discusses what triggers active conflict. It explains why conflict escalates from just being stuck to fighting – or from passive conflict to active conflict.

Family Factor – Chapter 6 will explain precisely why conflict in family business is so unique and how the strength of the family bond determines how well the family will be able to manage conflict. This chapter will describe how measuring the Family Factor enables us to predict if families will end up in litigation or other forms of extreme conflict and what can be done to avoid such an outcome.

Conflict Management Approaches – Chapter 7 will be familiar ground for those already well-versed in mediation and other forms of dispute resolution, such as litigation and arbitration. However, we will add two additional approaches not typically referred to as conflict management approaches: Development and Releasing Blame™. Development is the process of growing the family enterprise out of conflict, and Releasing Blame is a process most associate with forgiveness. We will show how these conflict management approaches work together to help manage family business conflict situations.

Interdependence – This component is a measure of the complexity of the overlapping roles among stakeholders in the family enterprise system. A mapping tool, The Stakeholder Map, will be presented in Chapter 9 that will help readers evaluate stakeholder roles. For example, if cousins are simultaneously owners, managers, and on the board of the family business, they have four overlapping roles, thus increasing the chance that they will have areas of disagreement. If they were family members only who shared no responsibility for managing a business, they would be less likely to butt heads. It follows then that the more Interdependence there is in a family business system, the greater is the potential for conflict.

External Factors – This component has already been discussed and refers to the various influences on the family enterprise that lie outside direct stakeholder control, but which can impact the level of stress and conflict in the system. They may include economic issues (e.g., interest rates or unemployment rates), or regulatory issues related to the specific business (zoning laws, environmental regulations or federal regulatory reviews). They may be related to global political stability, international market conditions, climate change, or competitor, customer or supplier consolidation. When external conditions are favorable, there may be less cause for conflict. When they are unfavorable and stress is higher and belts must be tightened, the potential for conflict may increase.

Once we have introduced and explained each term, we typically express that term as an abbreviation. For example, Interdependence will be expressed as "ID," External Factors as "XF," and Time as "t." In this manner, the general form of *The Conflict Equation* is expressed as:

$$C_t \propto \frac{\text{ID x Trigger x Reasons}}{\text{Family Factor x Conflict Management Approaches}} + XF$$

Key
C_t = Conflict over Time $\propto$ = is proportional to   ID = Interdependence
XF = External Factors

Figure 3-5

Thinking about how fractions work, take a moment to consider the impact of each of these components (or categories of components) on Conflict. If in the numerator there are many Reasons and Triggers for conflict in the specific family business system being considered, Conflict will be high. Similarly, if the denominator is high due to a strong Family Factor and effective, in-place Conflict Management Approaches, Conflict (or the potential for conflict) will be lower. Note also that while a small numerator will indicate a lower level of conflict, a low denominator will mean that the conflict is more likely to escalate.

Keep in mind that we are not looking for any specific answer or number. The purpose of the equation is only to better understand how each component of conflict interacts with every other component and how they all work together to increase or decrease (escalate or manage) conflict.

The key question to ask when using this equation is "will a change in any specific component increase or decrease conflict?" In order to answer this question, however, we need to go through the equation and fill in all the terms. In the coming chapters, we explore all these component categories in depth.

The Conflict Equation will help readers identify the underlying reasons for conflict, what triggers active conflict, how the strength of the family bond helps to manage conflict (or how its weakness drives the system to litigation) and what can be done to develop the family and its enterprise out of conflict. It also shows that not everything is controllable by stakeholders because the system is dependent on external factors outside of its direct control.

Summary

- *The Conflict Equation* provides a logical organizing structure to *understand and manage*, not resolve, systemic conflict.
- The equation is intended as a way to simultaneously consider the relationships of the individual components to each other and to provide insight into how altering one variable will affect the overall level of systemic conflict. These components can be economic or emotional.
- No numerical values are assigned to the variables – *The Conflict Equation* is a qualitative measure.
- The components of conflict are individually represented in *The Conflict Equation*.
- The equation can get family business stakeholders "unstuck" by helping them understand where the conflict in a family business system is coming from and providing a roadmap for how it can be reduced.
- While we provide an algebraic equation as a shorthand approach to help you employ the methods outlined in this book, think of the equation as a checklist to help you assess the complexities of systemic conflict, and the potential for improvement, in a family enterprise system.

Chapter 4

Deconstructing the Reasons for Conflict

Man must evolve for all human conflict a method which rejects revenge, aggression and retaliation.
— Martin Luther King Jr.

There are three underlying reasons for any conflict, be it in a family business or in any other situation where individuals and groups interact.

The Three Underlying Reasons for All Conflict
- Opposing Goals
- Incompatible Values
- Historical Impasse

Is it really possible that the reasons for all conflicts of every type can be summed up in only three categories? After all, conflict is caused by many diverse factors. So how do these translate into just three categories?

When evaluating conflict in a family business, it is important to identify as many of the underlying reasons why conflict exists in the system as possible. We introduce these three categories as prompts to get advisors and stakeholders to think about and categorize all the reasons that may exist. Thinking about the reasons for conflict through the lens of these different category types will generate the most complete inventory of reasons.

Even more important than simply helping create a comprehensive list of reasons for conflict, each of these categories of conflict demands different approaches to managing the conflict issues within those categories. This will be explained in greater detail in Chapter 7.

The way that these underlying reasons for conflict are treated in the equation is important. These three components are added to each other.

Reasons for Conflict = Opposing Goals + Incompatible Values + Historical Impasse

Our equation, therefore, expands as follows:

$$C_t \propto \frac{\text{ID} \times \text{Trigger} \times (\text{Opposing Goals} + \text{Incompatible Values} + \text{Historical Impasse})}{\text{Family Factor} \times \text{Conflict Management Approaches}} + \text{XF}$$

Key

C_t = Conflict over Time $\propto$ = is proportional to   ID = Interdependence
XF = External Factors

Figure 4-1

Or, using abbreviations:

$$C_t \propto \frac{\text{ID} \times \text{Trigger} \times (\text{OG} + \text{IV} + \text{HI})}{\text{Family Factor} \times \text{Conflict Management Approaches}} + \text{XF}$$

Key

C_t = Conflict over Time $\propto$ = is proportional to   ID = Interdependence
OG = Opposing Goals   IV = Incompatible Values   HI = Historical Impasse
XF = External Factors

Figure 4-2

A good way to think about these components is that they are different doors to the same room. The "room" is the category of "Reasons." Each door – Opposing Goals, Incompatible Values and Historical Impasse – is simply a way to enter the room with a certain mindset; a certain way to think about what is going on in the system. The objective is to fill the room up with all the reasons you can think of for why conflict exists in the family enterprise under consideration.

Although each of these reasons will be "tagged" as one of these three components of conflict, getting them into the room is more important at this stage than tagging them correctly. You may find that some of the reasons you have identified do not fit neatly into any single component category. The fact is that some reasons for conflict will involve values, goals, and history simultaneously. Also, someone might consider something a "value" while another might think of it as a "goal." The categorization isn't critical but getting the issue in the "door," any door, into the "reasons for conflict" room is what's important. Looking back to our earlier chapter on equations (Chapter 3), the ultimate sum of the components inside the "reasons for conflict" parentheses, not the specific number associated with each component, is what is important. The point is that looking for the underlying reasons for why conflict exists in the system through the lens of each of these categories helps you identify all the reasons in a useful manner.

> A good way to think about these components is that they are different doors to the same room.

Now, let's consider each of those components in more detail.

Opposing Goals

It is possible for stakeholders to have differing goals that are not necessarily in opposition. With enough resources, sometimes the multiple goals of diverse stakeholders can be realized simultaneously. Opposing goals are those that cannot be met simultaneously with the current set of resources available to stakeholders.

There are literally thousands of examples of how conflict over opposing goals is built into the family business system. For example, some family members may want access to wealth. Others may want a leadership role in the company or a controlling ownership stake in the business that has been denied them for various reasons. Family members working in the business may not want to keep paying dividends to family shareholders who are not contributing to the firm's success, while others may want the company to pay larger dividends instead of paying executives high salaries.

One example of opposing goals concerns a brother and sister who inherited a financial services company following their father's sudden, untimely death. The sister became very involved in the business operations and was the primary revenue generator for the business. Her brother, a very affable yet not particularly motivated employee in the customer service area, created very little of the generated revenue. The compensation plan that

> It is possible for stakeholders to have differing goals that are not necessarily in opposition. Opposing goals are those that cannot be met with the current set of resources available to stakeholders.

they "inherited" was developed when their father ran and owned the controlling interest in the business and the rising generation had lower-level jobs. That plan articulated that each family member was paid the same fairly low salary, and distributions of income were proportional to ownership. Since now each sibling owned 50% of the firm, they were essentially reaping equal rewards from their unequal service to the company. The brother supported the plan and asserted his contractual rights as the basis for his position. In contrast, his sister appealed to fairness to argue her case for a greater share of the income. Thus their goals for a revised compensation policy were clearly in opposition.

Typical Opposing Goals
- Company growth vs. status quo
- Pay dividends vs. reinvest for growth
- "I should be president!" vs. "No, I should be president!"
- Sell the company vs. retain ownership of the company
- "We should make the strategic alliance." vs. "We should not ally with that company."
- "Divide the foundation up." vs. "Keep the foundation whole because shared philanthropy will keep us together."
- Trustee control vs. beneficiary control

Incompatible Values

As described in Chapter 2, our values drive our goals and determine what we feel we need in our lives. Together with our unique personalities, our values define who we are. We may be religious or secular, Democrats or Republicans, conservatives or liberals, Type A or Type B people. We may or may not have a strong work ethic. The list can go on and on. Individuals and groups can coexist well when they have different values. However, sometimes values among stakeholders are incompatible and can serve as reasons that underlie conflict.

When in conflict, we call into question the honor and values of our adversaries. We ascribe to them labels like "greedy," "dishonest," "sneaky," "foolhardy" or "stupid." In these times, it is clear that there is more that fuels our battle than simply Opposing Goals. Adversaries in conflict may simply not like or respect each other. They may feel that they need to "win" to prevent the incompetence and corruption of their opponent from bringing ruin to the whole family.

The component of conflict that we call Incompatible Values is a large category. It can be thought of as a catch-all category for conflict reasons that do not fall neatly into the other categories of Opposing Goals and Historical Impasse.

Afflictions like alcoholism, for example, seem to impact family businesses disproportionately in part because a substance abuser may be enabled or shielded by his family position from the typical kind of consequences that would exist were he not at his family's company. A family member with a substance abuse problem is often a source of conflict in a family business. So, how would you categorize that issue in *The Conflict Equation* framework? As you get familiar with *The Conflict Equation*, you will recognize substance abuse as an Incompatible Value. Certainly, it has aspects of Opposing Goals – he wants to drink, the family wants him to stop. It may also have overtones of Historical Impasse – he did something in the past when he was drunk that was unforgivable. But the more important issue is that the alcoholic's addiction has set up an attitude regarding drinking or substance abuse that is incompatible with the family's values, or the expectations of the family workplace.

Again, labeling each reason correctly is less important than identifying all the reasons and getting them into the "reasons room."

Over generations, especially when one or more family branches have become geographically dispersed, "family values" developed in prior generations may evolve differently among branches. With marriages to different types of people leading to different child-rearing styles and perhaps different political or religious affiliations, families may develop very different value systems among their members. Differing values are not in themselves a threat to the family business system. It is only when these different values among stakeholders are incompatible – when stakeholders feel that they cannot coexist – that they can lead to conflict.

The concept of Incompatible Values covers a wide array of issues, including clashing personalities, lifestyles, and other values relating to family, business, and individual beliefs. Incompatible Values may evidence themselves as disrespect, dislike, inability to communicate among stakeholders, and may be perceived as existential threats to each party in conflict.

For example, in a family firm there is often a clash regarding risk tolerance that can significantly impede trying to find alignment on corporate strategy and policy. Imagine that one sibling is a risk-taker, and the other is risk-averse. They share leadership of the company and their differences in risk tolerance are the source of mutual ridicule and a mutual lack of respect. "Go big or go home!" vs. "Don't be so reckless!" are typically the words and sentiments underlying many of their arguments. This values clash leads to a communication breakdown between them, as they both feel they are incompatible partners and they are unable to decide how to move the company into the future.

When one group holds a bias against another for views or behaviors that are incompatible with their own values, conflict can grow.

Typical Incompatible Values
- Devoutly religious vs. atheist
- Pro-life vs. pro-choice
- "Children should participate in all activities." vs. "Children should be seen and not heard."
- Drinking alcohol is bad vs. everyone drinks
- Supports capital punishment vs. opposes capital punishment
- "Debt is a good way to fund growth." vs. "You should never borrow money."
- Democrat vs. Republican
- "Children should travel on our private plane." vs. "Children should fly commercial."
- "Trust funds encourage laziness." vs. "Trust funds allow for the pursuit of dreams."

Since values may drive goals, it is sometimes difficult to distinguish values from goals. For example, a goal to pursue a particular low-risk strategy may also be described as a value of low tolerance for risk.

Historical Impasse

Often, the description of a current conflict reaches back in time to historical resentments and grudges still held. Stakeholders in enterprising families have long histories with each other and often develop long lists of what they are owed, how they were wronged, and what is needed in recompense. From "Mom always liked you best" to "you took advantage of me," Historical Impasse abounds in families and underlies much conflict.

We often hear resentful stories of how in "Great Grandpa's generation," one or several siblings were denied ownership in the business. We may never know if, at the time, there were reasonable explanations for the decisions and actions that caused an impasse. Maybe the business was seen as very risky in the past and ownership was seen as more of a liability than a benefit. But now, the branch that took over the business has profited economically in comparison to the branch that stayed out of the business.

Regardless, over the generations, stories may abound about how "my grandfather" was cut out of his due, "my mother" was cheated by her older brother, or "Uncle Rob" was a swindler and practically stole the business out from under his younger brother leaving him only a fraction of its value. While such stories may be apocryphal, they carry the weight of family truths passed down.

Historical Impasse may have roots in more recent history. Siblings who work together may feel that the other was treated better, provided more support, and afforded more opportunity growing up, for example. Because stakeholders in a family business are likely to have a much deeper and more significant history with each other than stakeholders in a typical non-family, closely held firm, it is logical that they have collected significantly more impasses along the way, hold more grudges, and have more hot buttons to push with each other.

An Example of Conflict in Action

Two brothers started a restaurant business together. Tom had an associate degree from culinary school, and excellent experience working in restaurants in the area. He would be the chef. His older brother, Jim, had an MBA and had experience on Wall Street. He would be the business manager. Together, they invested some of their savings, got a loan from their parents, and set up shop. A local attorney drafted their founding documents, which assured them that all important decisions would require unanimous consent, and all profits would be split 50/50.

The business grew nicely. Within five years, the brothers had three restaurants spread throughout the city and profits were good. Based on this solid performance, Jim thought about expanding to other cities and upgrading their enterprise resource planning (ERP) system. Tom, whose reputation as a chef was beginning to grow, was feeling like he had achieved his goals and was content to reap the rewards of his efforts. He had recently married and had a child, and wanted to focus on his new family and a healthy lifestyle. Being the youngest in the family, Tom had grown up somewhat sheltered. He was never an academic star in school and did not have the opportunity to go to the Ivy League schools that his brother Jim attended.

Jim became more and more frustrated at his brother's lack of initiative. He had visions of going national with the brand they had built and he was working late most nights to see how this could be done. He was familiar with how companies finance growth and felt confident that they could achieve his vision.

Tom started taking time off to help with child rearing and house projects. He clashed with his brother over employee salaries – he wanted the company to be a great place to work for its employees. Jim, on the other hand, primarily wanted to improve profitability to attract investors and grow the brand aggressively.

In the end, they found themselves in constant warfare with each other. Because capital expenditures and distributions required a unanimous decision from the two brothers, they each were able to hold the company hostage. Company bank accounts soared as distributions and capital expenditures ceased. Morale at the company dropped, as employees saw the brothers battle every day.

To understand what is going on here, let's try to determine the underlying reasons for conflict.

Opposing Goals:
Jim wants to expand the company, perhaps bringing in outside investors.
Tom wants to stay small.

Jim wants to improve profitability.
Tom wants to invest in quality and improve working conditions.

Incompatible Values:
Jim is tolerant of risk.
Tom is risk-averse.

Jim is educated in corporate finance and believes this knowledge is valuable for decision making.

Tom lacks much of this skill set and doesn't think making decisions based on profit ratios is as important as whether they are achieving their vision of being the best in their class.

Historical Impasse:

Jim feels that Tom was always "babied" by his parents, while he, as the oldest, did most of the work and held most of the responsibility growing up. Tom owes him!

Tom feels that Jim was always favored by his parents. Jim got extra help when he needed it and no expense was spared to get Jim into the finest schools. Tom, on the other hand, was considered the "social" one and never given the support he needed to shine academically.

There are of course many more underlying reasons for conflict that can be dug out of this case. But this brief analysis shows how evaluating the conflictual situation from the perspective of these different categories reveals different aspects of the conflict, and gives us a more robust picture of what is going on.

We have identified six different reasons for conflict in the above example. That doesn't mean we put the numeral "6" in the parentheses in the equation. Keep in mind that the equation serves as a guide for the process of understanding and managing conflict. There is no purpose in using numbers for this equation, since we are not looking for a numeric answer. Rather, we are only interested in the list of *Reasons* that we have uncovered.

It can be useful to list these *Reasons* as accountants might make journal entries.

If it were possible to eliminate or reduce the intensity of some of these reasons for conflict, obviously, the conflict will reduce. That analysis will be the job of Chapter 8 and is the ultimate purpose of *The Conflict Equation*.

Summary

- There are three Reasons for Conflict – Opposing Goals, Incompatible Values, and Historical Impasse.
- Opposing Goals exist when two or more stakeholders have visions or objectives that are mutually exclusive, given current resources.

- Incompatible Values exist when one or more stakeholders define themselves or what is important to them in ways that are antithetical to other stakeholders.
- Historical Impasse refers to the personal or branch narratives that stakeholders bring into the present. We often think of this as the "baggage" that family members carry with them in the family enterprise system.
- Proper categorization of the reasons (i.e., calling something a goal vs. a value) is not critical – it is the identification of the tension that is important.
- No numbers are assigned to these components – they are qualitative measures that explain *why* the system is in conflict or simply stuck. A comprehensive list and understanding of reasons that underlie conflict is the only important result of this part of the deconstructing conflict analysis.
- *The Conflict Equation:*

$$C_t \propto \frac{ID \times Trigger \times (OG + IV + HI)}{Family\ Factor \times Conflict\ Management\ Approaches} + XF$$

Key

C_t = Conflict over Time	$\propto$ = is proportional to	ID = Interdependence
OG = Opposing Goals	IV = Incompatible Values	HI = Historical Impasse
XF = External Factors		

Figure 4-3

Chapter 5

The Trigger for Conflict: Disrespected Power

Power is a word the meaning of which we do not understand.
— Leo Tolstoy

There can be many reasons for conflict in a family business situation – opposing goals, incompatible values and historical impasses. But the presence of any of these does not guarantee that the family will be in active conflict. Without some event that sparks outright conflict, families experience only *passive conflict* that keeps them stuck, tiptoeing around each other for a long time. Conflict avoiders are familiar with the feeling of just looking the other way or developing "work-arounds" to avoid any confrontation that could lead to conflict.

There is only *one* thing that triggers conflict. Conflict is triggered by the exertion of power by one individual or group over another, in a manner that is perceived as without legitimate or moral authority, arbitrary, undeservedly punitive, or accomplished in a manner that is degrading or humiliating to the target of that power. We call this component of conflict Disrespected Power (DP). It is what triggers active conflict in a system primed for conflict, with ample underlying reasons for conflict as described in Chapter 4.

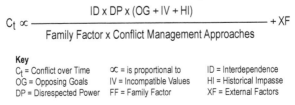

$$C_t \propto \frac{ID \times DP \times (OG + IV + HI)}{\text{Family Factor} \times \text{Conflict Management Approaches}} + XF$$

Key

C_t = Conflict over Time	$\propto$ = is proportional to	ID = Interdependence
OG = Opposing Goals	IV = Incompatible Values	HI = Historical Impasse
DP = Disrespected Power	FF = Family Factor	XF = External Factors

Figure 5-1

When stakeholders perceive that power in the family business system is held or used in a manner that is respected, there will be nothing to trigger active conflict – regardless of how stakeholders feel about each other, regardless of their individual goals, and regardless of their stormy histories together. Stakeholders may be miserable, they may dislike or disrespect each other, and they may be harboring deep resentments, but they will not have active conflict if they believe power is held and used in a manner that they respect – or, if power is never exerted among them in the first place.

Conflict is triggered by the exertion of power by one individual or group over another, in a manner that is perceived as without legitimate or moral authority, arbitrary, undeservedly punitive, or accomplished in a manner that is degrading or humiliating to the target. We call this component of conflict Disrespected Power.

Avoiding the exertion of power over others is akin to avoiding decisions that might impact others. When stakeholders sense that they are in a system that is rife with underlying reasons for conflict, they may seek to avoid conflict by reducing their interdependence; creating silos in the workplace so they do not have to interact or make decisions that affect each other. This reduction of interdependence also reduces the likelihood that they will be in a position to exert or be on the receiving end of disrespected power.

Disrespected Power: An Example

Mike, Alice, and Scott are siblings and second-generation owners of their family's manufacturing firm. Their father and uncle had a bitter feud in the prior generation and their dad bought out their uncle. To prevent such an outcome in their own generation, the siblings have learned to stay out of each other's area of responsibility. Alice manages the office, Mike runs sales, and Scott runs manufacturing. Mike is the oldest and his business card says "President," but they all operate as co-managers with equal salaries and equal, but separate, areas of authority. The business runs well, but the siblings never really discuss strategy and haven't made any significant investments in the business since they bought out their father twenty years ago. The last time they tried to talk about strategy, tensions rose when each revealed their opinion of how the other siblings' areas might change going forward. They left well enough alone, content to work hard and maintain the status quo.

Trouble is on the horizon, however. Alice's son William is a born salesman and has recently joined the company to work under Mike. William has new ideas and is becoming frustrated. Scott had some health problems and is looking to retire early. His kids are too young to join the business, but he wants to hold open the opportunity for them to join the business one day. Mike's daughter has been working in bookkeeping under Alice for a few years, and is frustrated that the company hasn't grown much and that there appears to be limited upward mobility for her.

"Siloing" worked to keep the peace for the siblings for many years. But it has also created a history of not talking and not planning. The needs of the incoming generation and the unavoidable transitions that must be considered for the siblings in the coming years will force them to communicate. If they avoid doing this, chaos will result. If they had been able to communicate, plan and manage the inherent conflicts that this would bring, they would have a more robust and resilient business and a better-prepared family.

> The distinction between how power is held and how power is used is important.

The distinction between how power is held and how power is used is important. A stakeholder may respect that his sister has a superior role at the company. He may understand that she earned her position and can get at least as high a position at another firm. However, when she treats him like her little brother at the office and teases him at meetings, it is how she *uses* her power, not the fact that she *has* power, that will trigger conflict. If she uses her superior position and the power that it provides in a respectful manner with her younger brother, conflict would not be triggered.

Types of Power

In order to better understand this term "power," we turn to the work of Bertrand Raven and John French, who wrote in 1959 about the five bases of social power. In their seminal paper, they wrote that power must be looked at from a variety of perspectives. We typically look at power as authority. Indeed, this is one type of power – the power of legitimate authority. However, in family business systems, there are additional types of power that stakeholders use to get what they want (or need).

The Power of Legitimate Authority

The organizational chart of a firm, the schedule of voting stock, the traditionally accepted roles of patriarch or matriarch in a family are all examples of where legitimate power is held. Holders of these positions of power have the "right" to cast a vote or to direct subordinates. The power they exert, however, can be disrespected when the recipient feels that the holder of this power has compromised the moral authority of his or her position, or when the right to such power was given or taken inappropriately.

When Legitimate Authority is Disrespected

The eldest son may have been given a leadership role in a family business, along with the attending advantages in compensation and control. A younger sister may feel unjustly disadvantaged by what she considers primogeniture bias, and feel that the position of power given to her older brother is illegitimate – given only because the brother was first in line. Therefore, this younger sibling, who feels disadvantaged, may not respect when her brother in the superior role tells her what to do or holds her accountable at the firm. This will trigger conflict when Opposing Goals, Incompatible Values or Historical Impasse are present. The fact that this situation exists may be a Historical Impasse in itself. Conflict is triggered when power is used from this privileged position; a position of legitimate authority that is disrespected.

The Power to Reward

Stakeholders in a family business may have several opportunities to reward themselves, as well as other stakeholders. Big salaries, perks, bonuses, promotions, gifts and influence are all examples of rewards. When the power to reward is used in a way that is perceived as biased, without merit, or against agreed-upon rules, that power may be disrespected by another stakeholder and conflict may be triggered.

When the Power to Reward is Disrespected

Rita and her daughter Sarah have always been close. There is an unspoken bond between them that is unlike the relationships that exist with her other children. Sarah never left her hometown and she leads a simple life. She is married with two children and a loving husband and she takes care of the house. She also spends a lot of time with her mother. She never used her art degree from college, although she occasionally sells some of her paintings at local galleries and fairs. Her brother Phil became a high-powered corporate attorney in New York. Considered the brightest of the children in the family, he is a shrewd investor and the go-to person in the family for contract review and business advice.

Rita recently went through an extensive estate planning process and had to select an executor for her will and a family trustee for her considerable wealth in trust. She selected Sarah, to Phil's astonishment and dismay – he was certain his sister didn't have the appropriate skills for the role. Phil was always jealous of Sarah's relationship with their mother, but this was the straw that broke the camel's back for Phil. Phil perceived the selection of Sarah as executor as a reward for her support of their mother – one he did not respect. He thought the decision should have been made based on the merits of who would have the most appropriate technical skills for the role. He decided he would no longer bend over backwards to help Sarah or Rita when they called for advice.

The Power to Punish

Withholding just rewards, benefits and acknowledgement; taking away privilege; or retaliating in a manner hurtful to another party are common examples of how conflict can be enabled or triggered through punishment. However, it is useful to point out that punishment does not always trigger conflict. Sometimes, the recipient of a punishment accepts the responsibility for an error that deserves punishment. The power to punish can have unifying results when exerted respectfully and perceived as justified (e.g., a well-deserved speeding ticket).

When the Power to Punish is Disrespected

Tim was again passed over for promotion by his father. His younger brother seemed to be the rising star at the company. At this rate, Tim was convinced that he would never rise past his position of being a middle manager at the family firm. He never would have joined if he knew that this would be his fate. When his wife, Anne, learned about this most recent snub, she announced, "That's it! He's never stepping foot in our house again. I

> Punishment does not always trigger conflict. Sometimes, the power to punish can have unifying results when exerted respectfully and perceived as justified.

don't care if he ever sees our kids again. Until he starts respecting you and giving you your due, I want nothing to do with him."

61

Tim was in a tough spot. He needed to keep peace at home, but he didn't want to start a war with his father. So, he kept his mouth shut and hoped it would blow over. The next weekend, Anne received a call from Tim's mother suggesting they come over to see their grandchildren. Anne launched into a rant, saying that Tim's parents were not welcome anymore. Anne has no power on the company's organizational chart, and no ownership rights in the business. However, she holds great power in the family because she controls her children's schedules and, thus, who has access to them. Tim's parents were aghast that Anne could stoop so low as to punish them in what they perceived as a barbaric manner. Anne's actions only served to escalate the conflict that was brewing between Tim and his father.

The Power to Connect

Sometimes power is found in unusual places. The salesperson who has loyal relationships with key customers may hold power far greater than his/her position on the organizational chart or ownership stake may imply. The same holds true for the family executive who has developed the trusting relationship with the bank and without whom continued bank financing may be in jeopardy. When stakeholders hold these connections hostage to force a particular outcome, it typically violates an expectation of trust and, thus, becomes a disrespected use of power and a trigger of conflict.

When Connectional Power is Disrespected

A daughter at a family trucking company was the VP of sales and had close relationships with most of the customers that rented trucks from their firm. At some point, an argument arose in the company concerning additional earned ownership and the daughter threatened to leave the business unless she got what she wanted. She effectively held the company hostage as she was able to use her relationship with the customers, and her threat to "take them with her," as leverage. This power was disrespected by other family members because they felt this was a betrayal of their family relationships, shared interests, and duty of loyalty as an owner, and conflict escalated.

The Power of the Expert

A stakeholder who, by expert knowledge, strength of personality or power of persuasion (i.e., expertise at managing people), may be the de facto leader of a company (or family) despite a subordinate title or role. Such a stakeholder is often at the center of a mutiny in a family business. When this individual holds the leadership of the company (or family) "hostage" by initiating or threatening a rebellion in order to force an outcome of some type, this leadership power is usually disrespected by some stakeholders and conflict ensues. This may happen when there is a delayed succession plan and the rising-generation leaders, who have already gained the confidence of much of the staff, begin losing patience with prior-generation leaders who won't "let go."

When Expert Power Trumps Legitimate Authority

The son of a very successful entrepreneur entered the family business with all the expected qualifications for providing next-generation leadership for the company. He received an MBA from a prestigious school and had more than a decade of experience and mentoring in the key areas of the business. In addition, he had plenty of success outside the family business to be credible in his own right. For almost ten years, the son's advancement in the business was stalled as the father refused to give up any control. Although the father had built the reputation of being the "heart and soul" of the firm, his leadership over the past several years had become erratic, arbitrary and, some felt, reckless. All eyes turned to the son for true leadership – even though the son had a subordinate title, no direct staff, no voting control, and no legitimate power. A mutiny ensued, pitting father against son – the power of legitimate authority versus the power of the expert.

When evaluating the family business, it is important to determine where power is held and how it is used. Looking at power from these perspectives (legitimate authority, the power to reward, punish or connect, and the power of the expert) ensures that all the key sources of power are considered. From this vantage point, discussions regarding how power is used (or threatened to be used) can uncover the need for learning how to properly exercise power (or refrain from its use) so that it does not trigger or exacerbate conflict. In addition, the recipient may need to better understand, cope with, and respect legitimate uses of power.

When Respectful Uses of Power Are Perceived Negatively

Being the target of someone else's use of power is often necessary for organizations to run smoothly and for groups to accomplish their shared goals. But it often does not feel good to be a subordinate in a given situation. This is especially true when the personal relationships between those exerting power and those who are the target of that power are strained. Sometimes family members develop behavior patterns, have knee-jerk emotional responses, or make assumptions about what others intend, and they may take on the role of victim. Even when extra care is taken to use power in a way that considers the target's feelings, and even when the relative positions of power are universally acknowledged as legitimate, sometimes the target of the power will react to that power in ways that might not appear appropriate or even rational. This is not to say they are never the victim of another's actions, but sometimes victimhood needs to be challenged. The target of that power may habitually say "There he goes again, lording his title over me as usual" – when, in fact, that is not what is going on from the perspective of the proverbial "fly on the wall."

It is important to reiterate that conflict in a family business is identity-based in nature. When a stakeholder feels that their identity is not being acknowledged as they expect it should, they do not feel safe. When this happens, the fight-or-flight-or-freeze part of their brain takes over and they are less able to think and react in a measured, well-thought-out manner. This will be discussed more in Chapter 10 when we discuss the psychology of family enterprise. The point is that how power is held and used is often subjective. By identifying all instances of disrespected power in the system, regardless of merit, we can better understand what is going on and begin to develop strategies to address these issues.

Disrespected Power as Conflict Trigger

Imagine that a stakeholder has dedicated her life to a career in the family business, getting the needed education, putting work ahead of her personal and community interests, and she sees her older brother (never a good student but always Dad's favorite) occupying the corner office just because he got there first (in her opinion). In the interest of family harmony, or because she's gotten used to this as a pattern of how things have worked in her family, she may be able to live with it.

But, suppose she has developed an initiative to create a new product line that, through her deep understanding of the business, she is confident will drive the growth the company needs. When she takes this proposal to her brother for approval, knowing it is the right thing for the company, instead of either giving the proposal the consideration it deserves or approving it because he trusts her judgment and experience, he dismisses it out of hand and races off to his golf game. This might be considered an act of disrespected power that triggers active conflict. Disrespect comes from many sources in this example. It comes from the fact that how the older brother came to hold power is not considered legitimate by the sister. It comes from how the older brother used power by dismissing his sister's proposal out of hand to rush off to play golf.

The Conflict Equation, thus far, shows that if individuals are not dependent on each other (i.e., Interdependence is zero) or if power is exerted among the stakeholders in a manner that is respected by the targets of that power (i.e., Disrespected Power is zero), active conflict will not exist. This shows that conflict can be avoided by separating stakeholders into "silos" so they do not need to interact, or by making sure that nobody makes any decisions that impact others. Clearly, both of these conflict avoidance strategies are antithetical to running a strong business or being part of a dynamic, successful family. Understanding the role of power in family business conflict is crucial so that stakeholders can navigate the difficult terrain of making decisions together as family.

Summary
- There can be reasons for conflict in a family system without any visible active conflict. There needs to be a trigger to ignite active conflict.
- Conflict is triggered when an individual or group exerts power over another individual or group in a manner that is disrespected. This can come from disrespecting the position of power or how that power is exercised.
- Understanding the role of power in family business conflict is crucial – where is it held and how is it used?
- There are several types of power which impact conflict in a family business setting:
  ◊ The power of legitimate authority,
  ◊ The power to reward,

- ◊ The power to punish,
- ◊ The power to connect, and
- ◊ The power of the expert.
- • It is important to determine where power is held and how it is used.

The Conflict Equation so far shows that Conflict over time is proportional to the level of Interdependence times the amount of Disrespected Power times the Reasons for Conflict (Opposing Goals, Incompatible Values and Historical Impasse).

$$C_t \propto \frac{ID \times DP \times (OG + IV + HI)}{Family\ Factor \times Conflict\ Management\ Approaches} + XF$$

Key

C_t = Conflict over Time	$\propto$ = is proportional to	ID = Interdependence
OG = Opposing Goals	IV = Incompatible Values	HI = Historical Impasse
DP = Disrespected Power	FF = Family Factor	XF = External Factors

Figure 5-2

Chapter 6

The Family Factor: The Most Powerful Component in *The Conflict Equation*

It is with the heart that one sees rightly; what is essential is invisible to the eye.
— *Antoine de Saint-Exupéry*

Strong family bonds are the best protection against the escalation of conflict. Strong families still sometimes have conflict, but they are able to manage that conflict better than families that lack a strong family bond. That said, strong family bonds can exist without affinity – families can place tremendous importance on their family ties, but they don't have to like each other. It can be difficult for an outsider to initially assess the strength of a family bond.

Further complicating this assessment, some families who profess love and devotion for each other in fact have only tentative bonds as a family. Conversely, other families in active conflict, with members who say that they truly despise their sibling, parent or cousin, may demonstrate over time that their bonds as family actually run very deep and that despite the current state of conflict, they would actually give their lives for another family member.

Our term for this component of conflict is, simply, the Family Factor (FF). Within *The Conflict Equation*, the Family Factor serves as a multiplier in the denominator, which gives it tremendous capacity to affect the equation.

$$C_t \propto \frac{ID \times DP \times (OG + IV + HI)}{FF \times \text{Conflict Management Approaches}} + XF$$

Key

C_t = Conflict over Time	$\propto$ = is proportional to	ID = Interdependence
OG = Opposing Goals	IV = Incompatible Values	HI = Historical Impasse
DP = Disrespected Power	FF = Family Factor	XF = External Factors

Figure 6-1

In this chapter, the Family Factor will be further broken down into its individual components. But we prefer to represent it as a whole concept in *The Conflict Equation* because of its uniquely important role in family business conflict. Breaking it down into its component parts helps us better understand and use this component to manage conflict, but talking about the Family Factor as a unique component, rather than its individual parts, is much more informative to our work in understanding and managing conflict.

The Family Factor is a measure of the strength of the family bond. It is determined by evaluating whether the family bond is strong enough to leverage compromise and a commitment to change. As we will see when we introduce initiatives to manage conflict, the ability for family stakeholders to compromise and commit to making changes that are useful in reducing conflict for the sake of family cohesiveness is a characteristic uniquely important to understanding conflict in family enterprise. This is the factor that illustrates the importance of the continuing relationships that we stress throughout this book.

> The Family Factor is a measure of the strength of the family bond. Is it strong enough to leverage compromise and a commitment to change?

Clearly, as the Family Factor increases, the whole denominator of *The Conflict Equation* grows. This means that conflict is less likely to escalate as the Family Factor improves. Conversely, if the Family Factor is very low (i.e., approaching zero), meaning that the family bond means so little to the stakeholders that they are not willing to compromise or make changes in order to preserve the family, then there is nothing to stop conflict from escalating to the point of litigation or worse. Remember that the kind of conflict we are dealing with is identity-based conflict. This can be among the most extreme types of conflict and when it escalates, the most extreme consequences can result.

So, back to the equation. Remember that dividing by zero is never permitted in mathematics. For our purposes, the Family Factor can become so small that it "approaches" zero, but never actually becomes zero. This is because families are families – whether by blood, legal structures, last name, or even if only in the perception of others. The only way that the Family Factor could be zero is if the family becomes non-family. (But then this framework would not be relevant.) So, for our purposes, the Family Factor can be very small, but it can never be zero. It's important to note that the smaller it is, the more the potential for conflict increases until it approaches infinity, because mathematically the outcome of any number divided by a much smaller number (i.e., almost zero) approaches infinity.

So, what, then, does infinite conflict mean? We define it as the potential for all-out war. When the Family Factor approaches zero, and the other elements of conflict exist (i.e., the numerator in the equation is not zero), stakeholders will go to great lengths to achieve the outcome they want – and take no prisoners in the process. This could mean litigation, cutoffs in the family, or even physical violence.

Deconstructing the Family Factor

As stated above, the Family Factor is a measure of the strength of the family bond and its ability to leverage compromise and a commitment to change. If stakeholders are willing to compromise and to change their behaviors in order to preserve and strengthen their family bonds, then the family will have more ability to manage conflict. Conversely, if they are not willing to sacrifice or compromise for the sake of being family, managing conflict will be more difficult.

How can the strength of the family bond be characterized? Think of it as a spectrum. On one end are families who genuinely care a lot about each other, and also care about remaining close in the future. At the other end of the spectrum are families who neither care about each other nor have any interest in maintaining relationships going forward. In between these two extremes, there is a range of families with a varying degree of Family Factor strength.

Some families have never been close but believe in the importance of their identity as part of the family even if they rarely see or communicate with each other. Others may want to maintain the fiction of being close or feel obliged to stay connected even if they do not relish the thought of actually spending time with each other. A typical family is made up of individuals and their respective relationships that span this range. Although we talk about Family Factor as though it is constant throughout a family, more often than not it is somewhat variable within families, as the Family Factor as a whole is a combination of many parts.

So what makes one family's Family Factor high versus another's low? In order to learn more about this highly important factor, we will deconstruct it into its component parts.

The Family Factor is composed of three key components:
- Shared history,
- Shared vision for being family in the future, and
- Trust.

Shared History

Shared history refers to the common experiences and memories that family members have. They can be positive or negative, happy or sad, or even neutral. Shared history can be kept alive through family stories and traditions and memorialized by photographs and home movies. Some families take pride in their history and it is important to them that the rising generation knows from whence they came and that they keep the traditions and shared experiences ongoing. Others live in the here and now and don't spend time learning about their ancestry, how they got to where they are now, or place much value in perpetuating a particular ethos.

A family that shares a robust and positive history together is likely to have a high Family Factor. This is, in part, because they have a solid foundation of positive memories and experiences together that serves to keep them naturally more aligned in their goals and values, making conflict less likely. But even more importantly, if they were unable to successfully manage conflict when it surfaced, they would have a lot to lose. At risk would be those fond memories of each other that would forever be tarnished by unresolved conflict. Having a strong, positive shared history among family members is probably the single most important protection against debilitating conflict that families can invest in.

Sometimes families are not storybook examples of harmony and "happily ever after." Sometimes they have difficult histories to contend with. They may have been challenged by substance abuse, bad behavior, messy divorces, bankruptcies, or tragic accidents of some sort and may not have many happy memories as family. But, to the extent that they have pulled together in adversity, they may have built a strong Family Factor despite these challenges (or maybe because of these challenges).

Family members may have very different experiences of their families. This is especially true when a family experiences a significant change in financial circumstances. Children growing up while wealth was being created might have experienced struggle and tough times. Younger siblings might have grown up after the family became more affluent. This disparity might serve to diminish shared history and, thus, lower its Family Factor. Age disparity alone may be a factor that diminishes shared history. In some families, older siblings may have left for college by the time the youngest ones entered grade school.

Families can also trick themselves into believing that their Family Factor is strong, only to find out that when conflict strikes, their families quickly devolve into the worst type of factional fighting. Take, for example, two different families that self-identify as being close in part because they vacation together every year at their seaside retreat. In one family, once they arrive each family member goes their separate way, spending time with their friends. They don't go to the beach, play golf or tennis, or spend unstructured time together as family. While they may travel together on the flights down and back, and share stories of the fun they had, their family vacations do not really serve the purpose of building a strong Family Factor.

Conversely, the other family gets to their vacation property and they plan fishing and scuba trips, beach picnics or hiking excursions through remote trails together. While they do see some friends while they are there, many nights are spent cooking meals, playing games, or just hanging out together.

On the face of it, both families vacation together, giving an outside observer (and themselves) the impression of closeness. However, the first family has only an illusion of closeness while the second family has developed much stronger, resilient relationships through the quality time they spend together. Anecdotally, when both families were challenged by conflict, the second family fared much better. They stood by each other during a severe market downturn, personal struggles, and significant transitions in leadership and ownership of their family company. In contrast, the first family collapsed into bitter litigation after the untimely death of the patriarch.

Shared Vision of Being Family in the Future

Having a shared vision of being family in the future speaks to whether or not family members believe they will remain connected over time. Some families are tied together through their ownership of shared assets while others have no legal ties but rather an interest in preserving their kinship across generations. When "being family" is important to family members, and when there is an expectation and desire for family members to remain connected and involved in each other's lives in the future, stakeholders have something to gain by investing effort in managing conflict well. Just as having a strong shared history contributes to a strong Family Factor, so too does having a shared vision for being family in the future.

Do family members share a common vision for being family in the future?

Inquiring into how individuals see the future of their family relationships can open up conversations about shared identity and vision. This can help assess the strength of the family's commitment to an ongoing relationship, and thus, their ability to manage conflict.

> When "being family" is important to family members, and when family members expect and desire to remain connected and involved in each other's lives in the future, stakeholders have something to gain by investing effort in managing conflict well.

Sometimes a family enterprise or shared wealth plays a central role in defining how families will preserve the family bond through succeeding generations. When a family business, or family philanthropy, serves as a focus for well-articulated family values and a structure for keeping family members connected, family members will have a very concrete vision of what "family" will mean in the future and how important it is. Families with such a legacy, or a lasting reason for being family, will likely have a strong Family Factor, as it is built into the structure of their family.

Some families may have a shared property passed down through the generations that has served as a gathering place for the family. Or, they may have strong traditions such as holiday meals, family vacations and retreats that keep them connected. If there is a proactive plan to maintain these structures and traditions, this can enhance a family's ability to maintain a shared vision for being family in the future. The danger, however, is that shared property, if not funded properly or organized well, can quickly become a source of conflict rather than connectedness. If this happens, participation in family vacations may wane as individual interests diverge and tensions increase. Even traditional family holidays can cease to be rallying points for family if succession is not considered (i.e., who will host Thanksgiving when Aunt Jane is no longer around?).

Properly organized for generational success, these traditions and shared vacation retreats can serve as powerful resources for strengthening the Family Factor. Additionally, when family members share hobbies and core values, they may simply enjoy being together and make time to continue getting together. Families of musicians, skiers, baseball fans and those who share religious or political beliefs may find camaraderie and true friendships within their families that they want to continue into the future. This will contribute to a strong Family Factor.

But, other families may stay together simply for immediate financial gain, personal need, or due to a sense of obligation. These family members may state that the family probably will not stay connected: "After Grandpa Stuart dies, we will probably just go our separate ways." Such a lack of vision about being "family" in the future will contribute to a low Family Factor and the family may not be as resilient in the face of conflict. They will not perceive that they have anything to gain through continued connection as family.

It could be argued that staying connected as family is not as important as it used to be. Generations ago, families stayed connected for basic survival. Individuals were judged based on their family heritage. Today, society places much more value on the individual. Greater mobility and mass communication have made relationships, especially family relationships, seemingly less important. In a world where we have thousands of "friends," is the importance of any individual relationship, especially family relationships, somewhat diminished?

Being stakeholders in an enterprising family forces family members to stay connected – perhaps longer than they might want to otherwise – to keep the enterprise running smoothly. In these situations, therefore, building strong family relationships, and a strong Family Factor, may be essential for the long-term success of the enterprise and the family.

Trust

Simply put, trust is the predictability that comes from knowing someone well. It is not a measure of affinity or shared goals and it is not necessary to like someone in order to trust them. It is also possible to love someone, yet not trust them, as many have, painfully, experienced. Trust is a critical component of family relationships, especially when it concerns shared economic or business interests. It is what enables people to make rational decisions beyond their own personal interests. Without trust, an individual can only make decisions that further their own self-interest. When trust exists, individuals can make decisions intended to further their shared enterprise, or their connected families.

> Trust is what enables people to make rational decisions beyond their own personal interests.

The concept of trust is often misunderstood in this context. Most people think of trust in the sense that they "trust" another person when they believe that the other person has their best interests at heart. We believe that this definition of trust is unreliable and fleeting because it depends on the situation. In some instances, a person may indeed "have your back." In other instances, the issue at hand may simply be too important to that person and they will choose their own self-interest over yours. In short, that definition of trust is one that can't be trusted (pun intended).

We view trust the same way that noted developmental psychologist Erik Erickson viewed trust when he described what he called the "first stage of childhood development." Erickson thought of trust in simple terms: predictability. When the newborn baby cries, he eventually learns to trust that he will be comforted. It is the development of this sense of the predictability of his small world that enables the child to transition to more advanced stages of development.

In a family enterprise system, therefore, trust is also akin to predictability. A stakeholder may believe that her brother is a drunk and a cheat, and that he will always look for ways to benefit at the expense of others. In our view, the brother can indeed be trusted. He can be trusted because the stakeholder group knows him well and can predict, with some degree of certainty, his behavior in reaction to decisions they may make. It is when stakeholders do not know each other well enough to predict how each will react to decisions that prevents them from functioning as a group.

This kind of trust is acquired through gaining an understanding of that other person; what they value, what they want, and how they operate. When stakeholders do not fully understand each other's roles in the business, and the concerns and motivations those roles encourage, or when stakeholders do not know each other well enough to understand each other's values and the behaviors that may arise from them, their actions can be perceived as unpredictable, unreliable and thus untrustworthy.

The Family Factor Continuum – Past to Future

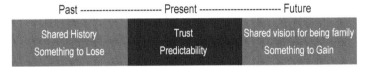

Figure 6-2

It is this sense of trust that connects a shared history to a shared vision for being family in the future. It is difficult to have trust if there is a limited experience of a person from the past. Even a negative history with a person is a basis for building trust. However, family members that have a very weak shared history with each other will be hard-pressed to find trust in their relationships.

> Trust is about predictability, not about whether someone will act in your best interests.

Similarly, when family members do not share a vision for being family in the future, they will also find it difficult to have or build trust. Even if their shared vision for being family in the future is that family connection will be minimal, that would be something on which trust can be built. It is the not-knowing that undermines trust because we trust people whose roles and values we understand, and whose behavior we can predict — at least to some extent.

Building the Family Factor

Understanding the Family Factor as a combination of the three components described above is a useful framework for determining the ability of a family to successfully leverage the strength of their family bond to forge compromise or expend the energy needed for, and accept the risks of, change. Each of these components is relevant to a family's appetite for managing conflict because if they have a shared history, they have something to lose; if they have a shared vision for being family in the future, they have something to gain; and if they have trust, they can make decisions beyond their own self-interest.

> Increasing the level of trust between family members may be necessary if raising the Family Factor is important for managing conflict.

As can be seen in *The Conflict Equation*, the Family Factor (a multiplier in the denominator) has a large impact on the level of conflict in a family enterprise – especially when the Family Factor is low. So, what strategies can be utilized to improve the Family Factor?

Building a Shared History

Sometimes family members in conflict have grown up in different places or, due to their age difference, had no overlap as children. While they may not remember spending time together as children, it is likely that they do have relationships with some common relatives – i.e., siblings in the middle or cousins who came to stay for a vacation or an extended period of time. Or, sometimes two siblings fifteen years apart in age may both have strong relationships with their parents. Geographically dispersed cousins may have close ties to their grandparents. Leveraging those relationships can stir up forgotten memories of common experiences or even similar memories of those middle siblings, parents or grandparents that create a tie between them. Shared history can be built by proxy.

There is not much a family can do to re-do the past, but it is never too late to try to reconcile different people's perceptions of the past. Some families have had a difficult history, complicated by feuds and historical impasse. The next chapter will discuss how historical impasses might be addressed. But, a difficult family history cannot be rebuilt solely by focusing on each of the specific incidents that led to hard feelings. When families have a negative shared history, but also desire to build their Family Factor, they can engage in a process of crafting a *new shared* narrative of that history together.

A shared narrative is not intended to cover up the past and recast a negative family history as positive. Rather, it is intended to acknowledge what happened in the past, honor the perspectives of all those involved, and articulate the lessons that came from the problematic past in a way that lays the groundwork for a rapprochement.

Building a Shared Vision for Being Family

A shared vision for being family in the future does not typically happen by itself. The process requires effort and needs to be proactive. Just as businesses create (or should create) succession plans and a corporate vision and mission statement, so too will families benefit from this same type of work.

Enterprising families who rely on having a strong Family Factor in the future should not leave the question of "who will host Thanksgiving after Grandma is unable" either unanswered or up to chance. Rising generations should be able to plan their lives with a reasonable understanding of the financial and career opportunities (and requirements for those opportunities) afforded by their family's assets. Family members should be engaged across generations to continually articulate what they stand for as a family and where they are headed. Family elders should pass down their stories and values to younger generations to provide the sense of the importance of family continuity. When being a part of the family for the future means something of importance to family members, they have strengthened their Family Factor.

Carving out time for family events that truly connect family members is the single best way to build resilience in the face of future conflict. When a family enterprise exists, and families are engaged in building that enterprise, they should remember that family enterprise is inherently conflictual and because of this, it is very important to build structures to enable a robust shared vision as a family.

Many successful families employ various structures to build connection as families grow in size and become more geographically, ethnically, culturally, and financially diverse. Family councils are an excellent way to formalize family decision-making and organization. Family websites and blogs (with appropriate security) are great ways to facilitate communication among and between generations. Shared philanthropy can also be used as a vehicle to keep family engaged. Family banks can help soften the realities of wealth disparity among family branches so that wealth is less of a barrier to family connectedness.

Building a shared vision for being family in the future may not seem important to some family members. When engaged in a family enterprise, however, where conflict is built-in to the very fabric of the system, building a shared vision for being family in the future is critical.

Building Trust

The hardest thing about building trust in families that have experienced conflict is overcoming the common preconceptions about trust.

False Preconceptions About Trust

- Trust requires affection for the other person.
- Trust means that the other person has your best interests at heart.
- Trust means that the other person would do what you would do in a given circumstance.
- Trust requires having respect for the other person.
- Trust requires being on the same side of an issue or conflict.
- Trust requires a belief in the honesty and integrity of the other person.

Once family members leave these ideas of trust behind, they can begin to build the kind of trust that is truly effective and reliable in families — predictability.

It must first be said that having a strong shared history engenders trust naturally. When family members have a solid understanding and experience of each other, trust simply exists. Likewise, when they have a shared vision for being family in the future, they are likely to be aligned in many ways and because of this, trust will likely follow.

People do not generally go from being trustworthy to untrustworthy in a short span of time. But sometimes, a family member may become unpredictable despite a robust shared history and shared vision, and then trust may be called into question. If this occurs, it indicates that something significant may have changed for that person. A family member may state that her brother has "changed, gone crazy, or maybe has a brain tumor" in her efforts to make sense of his new (i.e., untrustworthy) behavior. In general, digging deeper will unearth reasons for that person's changed behavior, and, when explained, trust can often be restored.

Take, for example, a case where the family member who lost the trust of his siblings turned out to have developed a substance abuse problem that he was hiding. His family members could not understand his new, secretive and unstable behavior. They never would have guessed what was really going on. Their trust in him was shaken and this was having terrible repercussions in the family business, since he was also one of the executives in the family company. Eventually, he was encouraged to share his challenges with one of his brothers. In addition, he joined a recovery program, and has been able to restore trust over time.

In another case, a family executive in the family business had lost trust with his family due to his changed and newly secretive behavior. It turned out that he was having a romantic affair. While that had a devastating impact on his wife and kids, the lack of trust caused by his newly unpredictable behavior severely compromised the ability of the executive management team to work together. Once he was able to share enough of what was going on with his wife and siblings, he was able to restore trust. Although there were still complications and ill-feelings, to say the least, predictability (i.e., trust) was restored.

In still another case, the erratic, unpredictable behavior of the patriarch was eventually explained by early-onset dementia. While this was a tragic ending for a dynamic, larger-than-life figure, his family could tell there was something wrong because his behavior and decision-making were no longer predictable. It is important to note that a loss of trust that once existed indicates that there is something wrong that needs to be addressed. Once that is understood, trust can usually be restored.

Summary

- The Family Factor is the most powerful variable in *The Conflict Equation* for managing conflict.
- A low Family Factor indicates a potential for extreme escalation of conflict, which could mean litigation or worse. When there is nothing to lose, nothing to gain and no trust (i.e., predictability), stakeholders will go to great lengths to pursue their own interests.
- The Family Factor is made up of a shared history, a shared vision for being "family" in the future, and trust.
- Shared history means that family members have something important to lose if they cannot manage conflict and risk splitting apart.
- A shared vision means that family members have something important to gain by managing conflict well and staying together as a connected family.
- Trust is defined by predictability, not necessarily by doing what's in another person's best interest.
- Trust enables a stakeholder to act beyond their own personal interest and for the greater interests of the family.
- *The Conflict Equation*:

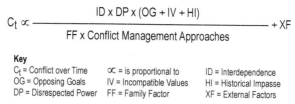

$$C_t \propto \frac{ID \times DP \times (OG + IV + HI)}{FF \times \text{Conflict Management Approaches}} + XF$$

Key

C_t = Conflict over Time	$\propto$ = is proportional to	ID = Interdependence
OG = Opposing Goals	IV = Incompatible Values	HI = Historical Impasse
DP = Disrespected Power	FF = Family Factor	XF = External Factors

Figure 6-3

Chapter 7

Managing Conflict

Our task is not to fix blame for the past, but to fix the course for the future.
— John F. Kennedy

Understanding how conflict in a family enterprise develops and gets triggered is useful, but understanding how to manage this type of conflict is even more important. Just as we deconstructed the reasons for conflict, we will now do the same for conflict management approaches. We divide these approaches into five avenues.

Conflict Management Approaches
- Dispute Resolution Approaches (DR)
- Releasing Blame (Forgiveness) (RB)
- Development Approaches
  ◇ Structural Development (SD)
  ◇ Personal Development (PD)
- Improving the Family Factor
- Adjusting Interdependence

Figure 7-1 illustrates where these conflict management approaches fit into *The Conflict Equation*. We will explain each of these in greater detail below.

$$C_t \propto \frac{ID \times DP \times (OG + IV + HI)}{FF \times (SD + PD + DR + RB)} + XF$$

Key
C_t = Conflict over Time $\propto$ = is proportional to ID = Interdependence
OG = Opposing Goals IV = Incompatible Values HI = Historical Impasse
DP = Disrespected Power FF = Family Factor XF = External Factors
SD = Structural Development PD = Personal Development DR = Dispute Resolution
RB = Releasing Blame

Figure 7-1

Dispute Resolution Approaches

There is a robust body of knowledge regarding dispute resolution, and a plethora of professionals who specialize in dispute resolution of one type or another. We will begin by introducing the two primary approaches that people most often associate with resolving disputes: the use of force, and bargaining.

There are two crucial points to make when considering force or bargaining approaches. First, both force and bargaining are dispute resolution approaches and are distinct from approaches for managing systemic conflict. Second, both force and bargaining can only address disputes relating to power, opposing goals, and some specific behaviors. One cannot use force or bargaining on issues related to Incompatible Values or Historical Impasse. That is, one cannot force or bargain with another to change his or her values, to like or respect them, or to truly forgive past events.

> Force and bargaining can only address disputes relating to power, opposing goals, and some specific behaviors. One cannot use force or bargaining on issues related to Incompatible Values or Historical Impasse.

Force and bargaining can, however, be used to change the balance of power, resolve simple disputes over money or possessions, and change certain behaviors. For example, force, or the threat of force, might actually be useful in getting people to the negotiating table where bargaining can begin. Additionally, the threat of force, or even a bargaining process of some sort, might be used to get stakeholders to engage with a family business consultant. Both of these examples show how force and bargaining might be used to change behavior – in this case, the behavior around managing conflict itself. Keep these points in mind as you continue reading about these approaches.

One additional thought to consider is that both force and bargaining are most easily effective when the issues are clear and between a very limited number of stakeholders or stakeholder factions – typically, two. Both force and bargaining approaches can become chaotic and potentially rife with unintended consequences when there are many stakeholders or groups in conflict, each with diverse interests.

Force

Using force, or the threat of force, is often what people in extreme conflict think of first. When faced with conflict, one party may evaluate whether force of some kind might be effective in trying to pursue his or her interests (i.e., perceived needs) over the interference of others. This evaluation will consider the type and magnitude of the power that is available to him in the current situation, compared to the power that his or her adversary has (or is perceived to have) in that situation. In theory, the individual or group that can exert the greater force will prevail, at least on some level.

In a family business, there is no shortage of power that stakeholders can bring to bear on other stakeholders. In Chapter 5, we showed how power can be considered from multiple perspectives: legitimate authority, power to punish, power to reward, power of the expert, and power to connect. When stakeholders are facing identity-based conflict, they will go to great lengths to explore every type of power they can throw at their adversary.

Stakeholders will use a rights-based approach like litigation or arbitration, for example, if they believe they can rely on the legitimacy of their position. They may threaten physical or economic force against their adversary, or the people the adversary relies upon, to further their position. They may bribe their adversary, or their agents, to get out of the way. They may withhold expert services or knowledge that their adversary relies on, or they may attempt to cut their adversary off from needed, or desired, connections.

Do not forget, conflict in a family business can be extreme. Power may be sought in areas that some stakeholders might deem off-limits. For example, as described in Chapter 5, the power to connect may include the willingness to withhold visitation rights between grandparents and their grandchildren. A sibling may threaten never to see the other again, or to never speak to a parent or child again.

> The use of force to try to resolve a conflict will most likely trigger additional conflict.

The problem with using force to try to resolve a family business conflict is that most often it is perceived by others as yet another example of Disrespected Power — the conflict "trigger" term we discussed in Chapter 5. As such, rather than improve a conflict situation, the use of force to try to resolve a conflict will most likely trigger additional conflict — at least during the time that force is being applied.

One could argue that as soon as one party prevails, the use of force will cease. Might it be worth the risk of triggering additional conflict *temporarily* if it led to a resolution of a dispute? The answer is that this is possible, but only if the conflict is truly a simple, isolated dispute. Remember, however, that most conflicts in a family business are systemic and complex. Using force to resolve a simple dispute might indeed be expedient, but it is likely that the dispute is related to other issues at play. Moreover, once the dispute has been settled through force (aka Disrespected Power), it is likely that the stakeholders on the losing side will forever consider that event as another Historical Impasse – adding yet another reason to the list that underlies continued systemic conflict for the future.

> Most conflicts in a family business are systemic and complex. Using force to resolve a simple dispute might seem expedient, but it is likely that the dispute is related to other issues at play.

Let's take a closer look at how different types of force can be used in a family business system.

Ability to Decide / Voting

Certainly one of the most direct uses of force to influence an outcome is when a system of voting or power-based decision-making is in place and used. When voting on an issue is possible, when a trustee or corporate officer has undisputed authority, or when someone in the family has clear moral authority regarding a decision, they may be able to force a binding decision. Voting or dictating outcomes from positions of power may be effective ways to resolve specific disputes. However, in a system where continuing relationships matter and where conflict is systemic, these power plays may produce more long-term harm than good. Voting or dictating decisions can be especially problematic when issues of identity are at stake. Being on the receiving end of a vote that challenges one's identity will no doubt raise the level of conflict among the affected group of stakeholders – despite its ability to check a particular dispute off the list. Today's forced resolution of a dispute may be tomorrow's Historical Impasse.

In addition, sometimes bylaws or policies specify that a vote must be unanimous in order to pass. This gives enormous power to a dissenter – essentially the ability to veto a decision that is desired by the majority. In some situations, this is as it should be.

But in others, relying on veto power can be a significant source of Disrespected Power.

In some cases, voting, or the appropriate use of legitimate authority, can be an expedient way of dispatching minor disputes that do not rise to the level of being issues related to the identity of stakeholders. When considering the use of voting or deciding, however, it is wise to make certain that the issues at stake are not perceived as existential threats to any individual stakeholder or to any important ongoing relationship.

The Impact of Time on Voting and Deciding

The good thing about voting or deciding is that it is immediate or, at least, quick. Not only is the process itself quick, but the impact of the process can be gauged quickly. It will be readily known if the result of the use of these types of force has triggered additional conflict or if it has served its purpose of resolving what turned out to be a simple dispute.

Litigation

In our litigious society, people often turn to litigation to resolve their disputes. In the courts, the presumption is that the side with the stronger, more legitimate argument will prove victorious. In practice, however, this is not always the case. Factual evidence is often inconclusive, and it is quite common that the best-argued case prevails, regardless of the facts. Outcomes, therefore, are unpredictable.

Even more concerning, however, is the fact that stakeholders who engage in litigation cede control over the outcome to this unpredictable process. Stakeholders no longer control their destinies when they choose litigation. They abdicate control of the outcome of the dispute to the courts and put themselves in their attorney's hands, letting him or her argue their case for them.

Another defining characteristic of our court system is that it is expensive and time-consuming. Due to its expense there is a built-in bias in favor of the parties with deeper pockets who can outlast their opponent. It is said that 90% or more of civil court cases actually never get to the judge or jury. Instead, these cases are settled on the courthouse steps in a hasty mediation that may succeed because the stakeholders are simply exhausted and going broke.

Even if a judge or jury decides a case, the outcome may not even be final. The appeals process can drag these fights on for years. Yet, despite many of these clear disadvantages of litigation, some stakeholders still insist on having "their day in court." Many, unfortunately, live to regret such a choice.

In addition, litigation concerns itself with fact patterns and legal precedent regarding very granular issues. While this may be suitable to help resolve individual disputes, this process is certainly not comprehensive or broad enough to address the larger systemic conflict. In a "just the facts, ma'am" process, for example, ongoing relationships are of little concern.

> Even the hint of litigation can be perceived as Disrespected Power and serve to trigger, or escalate, more conflict.

Finally, litigation, by design, polarizes adversaries and thus compromises continuing relationships. In fact, one of the first things litigators often tell their clients is to stop talking to the "other side" as it will only serve to weaken and compromise their case. You can imagine the impact this advice will have when given to family members who find themselves in dispute: parents and children, siblings and other family members put family on hold and take their seats on opposite sides of the courtroom. Attorneys have a very clear sense of who their client is and they aim to zealously defend and advance their client's "best interests." This generally translates to the client's "best economic interests." Attorneys have a fiduciary obligation to do so, and once litigation begins, they cannot violate this obligation for the sake of family relationships (with no tangible, measurable value) as they would risk being sued themselves.

Litigation also can be used to partially address Historical Impasse. However, while an economic solution to an impasse may be reached, it is unlikely that true forgiveness will be found through this process. The Historical Impasse will still exist, and may even be increased by the lawsuit itself, even though some remuneration has been won for a past violation.

It is interesting that even the hint of litigation can be perceived as Disrespected Power and serve to trigger, or escalate, more conflict.

The Impact of Time on Litigation

Do not underestimate the time it takes to litigate. Today's courts are crowded and it takes an extraordinary time for stakeholders to actually have their day in court. Litigants quickly find that time is money when litigators are involved. In litigation, the professionals in charge of the process have little incentive to make the process efficient and quick. And even when a decision is rendered, an appeal may add a whole new phase to this process.

Arbitration

Arbitration is a process whereby a private judge deemed acceptable to all parties is hired to resolve a dispute by evaluating the arguments and deciding the case. There are several advantages to arbitration over the court system. Arbitration is typically quicker, less costly, and final. Disputants can agree on binding arbitration such that no appeals process is allowed. In addition, disputants can choose an arbitrator with specific industry expertise or knowledge of a particular area of law.

Disputants can also agree in advance on the process by which arbitrators will decide the case. There are many arbitration processes (e.g., baseball arbitration) that have been developed to serve specific situations. While arbitration may offer less rigor regarding evidentiary process and discovery when compared to a court process, there are clearly many advantages to using binding arbitration to help resolve individual disputes.

Unfortunately, while arbitration provides stakeholders somewhat more control and influence regarding the process, the arbitration process, like the courts, requires that stakeholders abdicate control over the outcome to another – in this case, the arbitrator. This can be acceptable when the outcome of the dispute will not have a major impact on either disputant's life. However, when the dispute concerns an issue that is of fundamental importance to the disputant, leaving the outcome to another is taking a big risk.

Disputes in a family enterprise involve relationships as well as business or economic issues. When the decision is likely to impact an important continuing relationship among disputants, it is also a big risk to allow that relationship to hang in the balance of a third party's decision. Arbitration, therefore, may prove risky when continuing relationships matter and the issues are of significant importance (i.e., issues of individual identity).

Remember that in a family business, stakeholders may be deluding themselves into thinking that the argument is a simple dispute. Rather, it is more likely that the dispute itself may just be the tip of the iceberg of a systemic conflict that will escalate once the dispute resolution process has begun.

The Impact of Time on Arbitration

The arbitration process can range widely regarding time. Some complex arbitration processes can rival court cases in the time it takes to prepare, present and decide a case. Other arbitration processes can be completed more quickly. The outcome of an arbitration process, however, can have lasting negative impact on relationships among stakeholders.

Coercion

One might argue that threatening violence, economic ruin or holding certain important relationships hostage in order to achieve an outcome are forms of bargaining, not the use of force. After all, these threats may only be bluffing tactics. To the targets of the coercion, however, it feels like force is being used to achieve an outcome, and they will react accordingly. They will see these threats as yet more examples of Disrespected Power, and if successful, the issue may forever be remembered as a Historical Impasse among stakeholders.

Coercion may actually have a benefit over litigation or arbitration – it is within the measured control of the party using it. Unlike litigation or arbitration, control of the situation hasn't been ceded to others. However, because of this, it can seem more personal. Once a dispute has been taken to the courts, individuals can say, "that was just my lawyer talking – he has to say things like that." When stakeholders retain control, they cannot blame others for the process.

Coercion is typically used to force an outcome over specific disputes. It is not effective for making systemic changes or altering how stakeholders feel about each other and what they value.

The Impact of Time on Coercion

Like voting and deciding, threatening is quick and its impact can be gauged soon thereafter. If coercion simply triggers additional conflict, it is likely that the person using coercion as a tactic has misjudged the situation.

Bargaining

There are several forms of bargaining that stakeholders can use to try to resolve a dispute. Unlike the use of force, bargaining to resolve disputes in family business is more likely to be helpful and will certainly have a far lower chance of damaging relationships. Bargaining may be used hand in hand with the threat of force, as a lawsuit could be the result of a failed negotiation. Similarly, mediation or settlement talks can interrupt, delay or stave off a trial.

Like force, bargaining is a dispute resolution technique that, by itself, is not a robust approach for managing systemic conflict. This is because bargaining can only address issues of opposing goals, where power is held, how power is used, and, perhaps, some specific behaviors. One cannot bargain with their values, history, and their affection and respect for others. Simply put, people cannot negotiate or bargain with their identity, and since conflict in a family business is identity-based, bargaining is only of limited use.

> Bargaining is a dispute resolution technique that, by itself, is not a robust approach for managing systemic conflict. People cannot negotiate or bargain with their identity, and since conflict in a family business is identity-based, bargaining is only of limited use.

Negotiating, or bargaining, is a skill that, like other skills, requires both talent and training. Not everyone is equally adept at bargaining, and so the process of direct negotiation can often fail or produce unfair and imperfect results.

Bargaining has many advantages over the use of force for helping people resolve disputes. First and foremost, it keeps stakeholders in control of their destiny – they do not abdicate control over the outcome of their dispute to others, which makes it very attractive as a dispute resolution technique.

One of the most influential and important texts on negotiation is Roger Fisher and William Ury's best seller, *Getting to Yes: Negotiating Agreement Without Giving In*. It is a must-read for anyone interested in learning about interest-based negotiation. In *Getting to Yes*, the authors explain that it is crucial to focus on "interests" rather than "positions." Interests are the reasons behind positions – why individuals "need" the things that define their entrenched positions.

Another key insight from *Getting to Yes* is the importance of identifying a Best Alternative To a Negotiated Agreement (BATNA). Vetting out alternatives is key in any negotiation. The strongest alternative (i.e., what an individual can do on their own if the negotiation doesn't end in agreement) is what they can use as a measuring stick to assess the desirability of any option put on the table. So, if what is offered is less good than the best alternative, the stakeholder should walk away. If it's better, he or she should take the offer.

Good, effective bargaining to help address disputes in family business situations requires the elements listed below.

Conditions for Effective Bargaining
- Mutually acceptable rules of engagement
- Good communication skills
- Understanding of the relationships involved and the impact of any negotiated agreement on them
- Good emotional intelligence skills
- Relevant subject area expertise
- Problem-solving mind-set
- Availability of relevant, reliable data
- Clarity regarding each party's interests
- Understanding of each party's BATNA
- Open mindedness regarding "enlarging the pie"

Bargaining can be approached in two ways: direct negotiation and facilitated negotiation, popularly known as mediation, but also including the evolving practice of collaborative law.

Direct Negotiation
When stakeholders become disputants, it is common that emotions run high, judgment becomes clouded and inherent communication and information processing skills diminish. Add this to the fact that stakeholders generally have not been trained in negotiation in the first place. They may have never heard of *Getting to Yes*, or any of the other frameworks and tools that professional negotiators have studied. While stakeholders may be the most passionate advocates for their positions, this passion can get in the way of successful negotiation.

One of the most common reasons for the breakdown in direct negotiation is the difficulty disputants have in gaining the perspective needed to understand the interests that underlie their and their opponent's positions. It is easy for disputants to get so caught up in arguing for a specific position – a number that may represent salary, the value of an asset, a specific time frame, an event, or a specific behavior – that they may lose sight of the actual interests that their positions are intended to meet by those positions. It is likely that their underlying interests could be met in a variety of ways but, once positions harden, it is extremely difficult for disputants to backtrack.

Disputants in direct negotiation might consider hiring a trained facilitator who can challenge them regarding their articulated positions and help them better understand the interests that lie behind these positions. The facilitator also can recognize the disparity in negotiating skills and help level the playing field as the direct negotiation process can favor the disputant with better skills or a stronger personality. Similarly, disputants might consider hiring individual conflict coaches to help them better understand the negotiation process so they can negotiate more effectively.

Facilitated Negotiation: Mediation

The most common form of facilitated negotiation is mediation. A mediator is a trained neutral who helps all parties in dispute to voluntarily resolve that dispute in a way that is acceptable to them. It is the mediator's job to ensure that all parties have a voice at the table and are heard. In this way he or she can help level the playing field regarding the negotiation skills and relative power of each disputant, while making sure each is fully informed and neither is being coerced. A mediator does this through a combination of active listening, coaching, education, and facilitated discussion.

There are many different types of mediators, each with different philosophies, skills and abilities. Some are topic experts and, while they do not take sides, they can provide some degree of perspective that may be helpful to the parties in dispute. Other mediators eschew this practice and believe that their role is only to facilitate conversation and to avoid providing any topical information or ideas that do not come from the disputants themselves. While there is no "correct" approach or style, parties must consider the different types of neutral experts and decide what type of professional will best meet their needs.

Good mediators have excellent listening and reframing skills. Reframing is a process practiced by mediators where they repeat back the substance of what they heard, but with neutral language and within the broader context of the discussion. Through this process they help all disputants better understand the underlying interests that drive each of their articulated positions. This may help disputants consider alternative approaches to advance their interests and that move them beyond the positions they previously hung onto so tightly. In addition, mediators can help disputants get a clearer understanding of their BATNA, which helps them better evaluate potential agreements. A mediator may also coach parties to explore options they had considered previously that might enlarge the pie and provide "win-win" solutions.

In order to engage in a mediated process, disputants develop and sign an agreement to mediate. This is a declaration of their intent to seek a voluntary mediated solution, an outlining of the process that has been agreed to, and a description of the role and liability limitation of the mediator. These agreements also have confidentiality clauses, the intent of which is to prevent any of the mediation proceedings from being used in a court case should the mediation fail to achieve a settlement. Mediation is an alternative to litigation, but it is not intended to interfere with the ability of parties to litigate should the mediation process break down.

The result of a mediation may be a written agreement including a set of terms to be memorialized in a document (a memorandum of understanding) that each party can rely on. If desired, the memorandum could be drafted into a legally enforceable contract that would be signed by all parties. Alternatively, parties may prefer to leave the mediation with simply a greater understanding of each other's interests or with their agreed-upon next steps, and may not need a written agreement.

Collaborative Law

Another type of facilitated negotiation is the practice of collaborative law. In this consensual dispute resolution process, each disputant hires an attorney who will support them directly while exploring the joint interests of the parties. The attorney will advocate for their own client's interests while developing a mutually agreeable resolution. To incentivize a collaborative, negotiated settlement, the parties agree at the start of the process upon a protocol for sharing information, and an agreement that information found through the discovery process can only be used in litigation with the consent of the other party, should a negotiated settlement not be found. They also agree that all substantive experts are jointly hired and agree not to testify for either side should the matter go to trial. This structure avoids a costly "battle of the experts" and enhances a robust interaction between the expert and clients. The disputants further agree that their attorneys and respective law firms would be prohibited from representing them in litigation in the event that they fail to achieve a negotiated settlement. This would dramatically raise the cost of a subsequent litigation process and therefore incentivizes agreement.

A benefit of collaborative law is that, when it works, the parties can develop flexible settlement arrangements at the same time that they preserve both their ongoing relationships and their privacy. Their attorneys' only economic interest is to achieve a settlement that the parties have a vested interest in upholding. In addition, it provides each adversary with a skilled advocate who understands the legal principles at hand and who can educate and guide their client in these legal matters.

This process aligns the interests of the client and attorney and drives the system towards a negotiated settlement that can remain private. It removes the financial incentives for attorneys to drive clients toward expensive litigation or for clients to maintain a positional stance. In this process, each disputant has a skilled advocate who teams up with his or her client to collaboratively resolve a dispute with the other side.

Consensus Building

Consensus building is another interest-based dispute resolution technique that is effective for aligning multiple stakeholders with disparate interests. Allowing each individual's interests to be voiced and explored, the consensus-building approach develops inclusive solutions that allow the group to move forward without alienating any party or parties. The process puts the responsibility for moving ahead (or not) with a particular course of action on each individual. For any given option supported by members of the group, a dissenting party must articulate how that option would need to change to be acceptable to him or her. Through a process of give and take, the group continues to refine their proposals until all can buy into a solution. While this can take considerable time and effort from all involved, the end result leaves all parties feeling heard and fairly treated.

Impact of Time on Bargaining

While the duration of any bargaining process varies, it can last anywhere from hours to months. The time needed to identify the underlying interests of each stakeholder and to develop options to meet those interests will vary depending on the complexity of the issues and emotions at play. In addition, as the mediation process progresses, the disputants may learn things of which previously they were unaware. As mediators reframe and summarize positional statements into interests, new options for moving forward may come to light. Mediation typically proceeds at the stakeholders' desired pace as they are in control of the process and the outcome. Outcomes are typically reliable for the long term because they have been arrived at mutually. However, even the best outcomes are likely to be related to specific disputes, not systemic conflict, and systemic issues likely will continue to cause conflict in the future.

Releasing Blame

In Chapter 4, we discussed the reasons for conflict and introduced the component of conflict called Historical Impasse, generally disputes from the past that have not been resolved and continue to impact present-day relationships. In order to get beyond these past hurts, a process of forgiveness must be gone through by those affected.

Forgiveness rituals lie at the heart of all major religions because forgiveness is so central to maintaining important continuing relationships. Forgiveness is also a term that means different things to different people, and for which there is no shortage of theories and techniques developed for how it can be achieved.

We see forgiveness as the process for moving on in one of several ways. Note that we don't propose that one can or should "forgive and forget," because we really haven't seen anyone "forget" serious transgressions. Rather, it is blame or victimhood, and the anger it drives, that stands in the way of so many continuing relationships, and therefore exacerbates and prolongs systemic conflict.

One process for releasing blame that is particularly useful for family relationships comes from the book *How Can I Forgive You: The Courage to Forgive, the Freedom Not To*, by Janis Abrahms-Spring, PhD. Although Dr. Spring wrote her book primarily for married couples who want to stay married despite a serious transgression such as infidelity, it is an effective framework because Historical Impasses that develop in family business can feel, to stakeholders, akin to that level of betrayal.

In her book, Dr. Spring identifies four choices one can make regarding forgiveness (see the list below).

Types of Forgiveness

Refusing to Forgive: Yes, this is a choice.

Cheap Forgiveness: Forgiving because it's supposedly good for you, or because you feel compelled to by your religion or community norms.

Genuine Forgiveness: A process requiring equal vigilance from both sides, involving introspection, communication, and development of a shared vision for a continuing relationship.

Acceptance: Acknowledging your contribution to the impasse and forgiving yourself, and accepting a compromised relationship with the transgressor.

It is not an oversight that "apology" is not specifically mentioned in the above list – and it's not because love means never having to say you're sorry. The role of apology in forgiveness is complicated. A misguided or superficial apology can often make matters worse. Yet the right apology, at the right time, within the context of genuine forgiveness can do wonders for the reestablishment of stalled communication.

> The key to being able to release blame in a family enterprise is for all parties to an impasse to acknowledge their own contribution to the impasse and reaffirm the importance of the relationship that was damaged.

Likewise, reparations, like throwing money at a problem to make it go away, can deepen an impasse if they are seen as adding insult to injury. Or, reparations can be the grease that moves relationships beyond impasse.

The key to being able to release blame in a family enterprise is for all parties to an impasse to acknowledge their own contribution to the impasse and reaffirm the importance of the relationship that was damaged. Creating a shared narrative, as was discussed in Chapter 6, can be useful in helping a family integrate an impasse as a learning opportunity or as a turning point in their family history that provides the basis for continued relationship.

The Impact of Time on Releasing Blame

Forgiveness, or the releasing of long-held blame, can take a very long time. However, sometimes just the realization that there is a process to move away from blame and to achieve forgiveness (or even a level of acceptance), takes the edge off long-held grudges. Similarly, recognizing that refusing to forgive is a choice can help the process. When faced with a choice of maintaining a grudge and having to go through an uncomfortable, highly emotional forgiveness process, we find that some stakeholders gain enough perspective from simply learning about forgiveness choices and process that the old grudge seems less urgent and less important.

Development Approaches

Force and bargaining may be effective methods for resolving current disputes regarding opposing goals and how power is held and used. A forgiveness process may be useful in resolving historical impasses. As such, they may contribute to managing conflict, but they are not sufficient. Moreover, when these techniques are used in isolation, rather than being part of an overall conflict management strategy, they can be counterproductive. The power of Development, however, is unrivaled as an approach to managing systemic, identity-based conflict in enterprising families.

Development is the process of growing, not forcing or negotiating, the family and its enterprise out of conflict. Development has the broadest impact on the components of conflict and can be used to grow the Family Factor, align goals, diffuse values incompatibility, and even manage where power is held and how it is used. In order to properly consider how Development can be used in a family business system, it is useful to further deconstruct Development into its component parts: Structural Development (for both family business and family wealth), and Personal Development.

Although the term "Development" is not typically associated with conflict management, there is a wide variety of professionals involved in development for family enterprise who are often called when conflict arises. Consultants, coaches, attorneys, CPAs, CFPs, therapists, educators, and even clergy are some of the professionals who help organizations, groups, and individuals improve their structures, skill sets, planning, and self-awareness so that they can grow or evolve out of conflict.

In order to put Development into context, consider that conflict in an organization plays a similar role to fever in a human being's physical system. It tells us that something is wrong that needs fixing. *The Conflict Equation* will identify what is causing and triggering conflict, as well as why the family is having difficulty managing conflict. Finding development opportunities that address each of these components of conflict can be the most effective approach for managing conflict.

Structural Development for Family Business

How an organization is structured, and how that organization develops and carries out its mission, may inadvertently and needlessly enable or trigger conflict. The structure of organizations can be understood and evaluated by examining the following:

- Company Organizational Chart (with family members noted)
- Company Bylaws and Charter Documents
- Employment Agreements and Hiring Policy
- Employee Review Policy and Process
- Job Descriptions and Compensation Policy
- Shareholder Agreements, Ownership Schedule and Voting Rights
- Board of Directors Structure and Policies
- Operations Policies and Procedures (e.g., ISO 9000 Manual)
- Statements of Mission, Values and Vision
- Strategic Plan and Strategic Planning Process
- Cash Flow and Capitalization (Company Financials)

When looking through each of these windows into the structure of an enterprise, many ways to improve the system may come to mind. But, trying to improve the structure of an organization for its own sake, or because doing so comports better with some best practice that has been promoted, can actually be counterproductive in a family business if its impact on the system is not well-considered. Substituting best-in-class employees at every level of the company, for example, may certainly improve operations. But, when those employees replace family members, thereby destabilizing family equilibrium and relationships, the results may be catastrophic.

Specific areas of development should be investigated for the purpose of addressing specific components of conflict that were identified in *The Conflict Equation* process.

For example, there may be Opposing Goals regarding which members of the next generation should be welcomed into the company. There may be Incompatible Values concerning the evaluation of a family member's worth to the company. Family employment policy and family employee review policy might be Structural Development opportunities to address these components of conflict.

> How an organization is structured, and how that organization develops and carries out its mission, may inadvertently and needlessly enable or trigger conflict.

Structural Development for family business can put in place policies that encourage objective decision-making and discourage conflicts of interest. Structural Development is particularly useful in addressing where power is held and how power is used – i.e., the Trigger for conflict. When power is codified by agreed-upon policy and process, conflict triggers might be avoided.

Developing each functional area of an enterprise with an eye towards increasing professionalism and transparency, eliminating bias and conflict of interest, and improving efficiency can have a direct impact on the level of conflict in a system. Among the professionals in a position to address these issues might be the company's corporate counsel, CPA, general business consultant, and family business consultant. These advisors can make recommendations informed by relevant best practices in the governance and operations of a business.

All-family boards, even when members have excellent business skills and experience, can be counterproductive when family members are in conflict, as they can quickly devolve into branch factionalism and politics. If ownership becomes fragmented and knowledge of the business and industry is limited, an all-family board may be unable to determine what is best for the business or how to decide on distribution policies, thus perpetuating bad practice to the detriment of both the business and the family.

Structural Development for Family Wealth

Structuring family wealth so that conflict is well-managed is especially important for families that are new to wealth. In the book *Strangers in Paradise: How Families Adapt to Wealth Across Generations*, author James Grubman makes the analogy that families who are new to wealth are like immigrants to a new country – with a new language, a new culture and new rules. How they integrate into that new world, and relate to their children and grandchildren who, having grown up affluent, are like natives to this land, is a very difficult challenge for families.

The liquidity event that propels some families who sell their business and enter this new land of wealth requires significant planning and development of structures to help them successfully navigate this new world. Although it can be uncomfortable, families may recognize that their long-standing trusted advisors might not be capable of managing the newly increased complexity in their affairs. This is not to say that their skills can't be supplemented by those of other professionals, but families may need to hire new or additional advisors such as trust and estate attorneys, investment managers, insurance brokers, and accountants, among others. Building the financial support structures appropriate for their level of wealth will help them manage conflict over time.

Statistics show that there will be over $30 trillion in wealth transfer in the coming decade – and the highest amount of wealth contained in trust that there has ever been. Whether a family is transitioning to new wealth, transitioning to a new generation of control over wealth, or experiencing a crisis or conflict over wealth, how wealth is structured can have a tremendous impact on how conflict is managed.

The following structures are typically used for managing and transitioning wealth:

Banking and Investment Accounts
Insurance
Loans

Direct Investments, Venture Capital
Trusts (an alphabet soup of different types)
Philanthropic Entities (foundations, donor-advised funds)
Family Banks (a type of trust)
Material Possessions and Property (real estate, art, jewelry, etc.)
Wills
Verbal and Written Contracts

When considering these structures, it is important to evaluate each one for the following qualities to ensure that it is not a source of conflict:

1. Is each entity being managed competently, with no conflicts of interest?
2. Is there clear direction for the management of each entity that is in line with family and individual values and goals?
3. Is there appropriate transparency and access?
4. Does each serve a well-articulated purpose for the family or individual?
5. Do lifestyles seem sustainable and/or commensurate with the level of wealth and liquidity?

When managed and set up correctly, wealth can be a great resource for managing conflict. But, wealth also represents power and can thus trigger conflict when held or used in a disrespected manner.

When considering how wealth structures can be an approach to managing conflict, consider first which components of conflict might be addressed by wealth. With enough wealth, properly deployed, perhaps some opposing goals can be mitigated. If two siblings are qualified and want to lead the family company, perhaps an investment can be made in another venture for one of them to lead. Wealth disparity among branches can lead to other opposing goals, like where to go for family vacation and incompatible values like what is appropriate for Christmas gifts. A family bank, a trust with specific guidelines for how, when, and which beneficiaries can access funds, can be set up to articulate guidelines that help manage wealth disparity within a family. For example, family bank funds could be available to provide for health care, education, and under certain circumstances seed capital for an entrepreneurial venture. Funds also could be used to pay for family trips or whatever other types of expenses the family wants to cover.

Family Councils

For families wanting more structure and involvement in family decision-making, a family council can provide that more formal organization. In simple terms, a family council is composed of a group of family members who want to organize family activities — be they holiday gatherings, annual retreats, communications or, in the case of business-owning families, business status and performance review sessions. For business-owning families, the family council may have the ability to appoint a family member to the company's board of directors. In this way, the business keeps informed of family needs, developments, and general interests, and the family is kept current with the business issues.

Depending on the size, geographic dispersion, and complexity, the family council may meet regularly by phone, video, or conference call. While these meetings should have an agenda, they will vary in formality depending on what family members want. Some family councils ask their advisors to present information at their meetings, or have these meetings facilitated by a neutral party.

It doesn't have to be an onerous task to develop a family council nor does it have to be a rigid organization with lots of policies and protocols – unless that's what the family wants. Most families start small and agree on the purpose for the council or develop a family strategy. Often, the purpose is to organize annual or semi-annual family get-togethers or reunions for the purpose of providing opportunities for cousins to spend time together. In other cases, especially when there is a family business or significant shared assets, there will be times set aside for a business meeting where performance is reviewed and distributions are discussed. At these meetings, younger family members may participate in educational programs, often including wealth or philanthropy topics, which will also transmit family values and mission.

Highly structured family councils often develop a family constitution, which articulates a family's mission and values, and perhaps a vision for how the family will contribute to society. Some families we work with adopt a family constitution that articulates the family's purpose, mission, and values. These can be read aloud at the start of each family meeting so that all members are reminded of what the family stands for and wants to perpetuate in the future. These are living documents, evolving as families evolve. In these ways, families commit to their ongoing relationships and shared activities for the future.

Personal Development

When stakeholders in family enterprise perform well in their roles, communicate appropriately with other stakeholders, have good dispute resolution skills, have values that comport with their organization's values as well as the values of other stakeholders, are aligned in what they are all trying to achieve together, and, most importantly, are empathetic to each other, conflict can be managed well. The process of building these skills, aligning values and goals, and nurturing empathy is what we call Personal Development. It begins with the individual stakeholder, but eventually involves the development of groups of stakeholders together.

Personal Development may involve personal coaching, education, specialized experiential learning programs, or psychotherapy — whatever is needed to develop an individual in a way that allows them to better understand and participate in the family enterprise system. For example, Personal Development can help stakeholders work on issues of self-awareness, improved communication, conflict management skills, evolution of personal values, awareness/acceptance of the values of others, as well as issues related to mental health, or alcohol and substance abuse. Financial literacy education and learning about the family's heritage and legacy can be especially effective ways to manage conflict over shared wealth and business. Unlike dispute resolution techniques, Personal Development work can specifically address Incompatible Values and build the Family Factor. In addition, this work can even address Opposing Goals and how power is used, as stakeholders become more aware of and empathetic to each other.

Take, for example, a family where substance abuse (alcoholism specifically) caused problems. Ryan, a cousin working in the business, had an alcohol problem that had ebbed and flowed over time. He was generally able to function well at work, although some days he came in late or was nasty to his co-workers. His colleagues knew that due to his status as a family member, he would not be fired for poor performance or bad behavior. Some complained to management about Ryan, and the managers (most of whom are family members) became increasingly frustrated.

While Ryan's role at the company was problematic, a look at the family's history told a more complicated story. Alcoholism was present in the prior three generations. Family lore recounted "funny" stories of Great Grandpa and his friends' drunken adventures. Grandpa was known to have passed out at numerous family events, while being lauded as "the life of the party." Uncle Jack, one of the company's top salesmen, was known to have a few too many at business meetings and on sales trips. By re-framing Ryan's issue as a shared family problem, not as just his own personal failing, the family realized that this affliction could manifest next in one of their children, or even in themselves.

So, rather than continuing to point their fingers at Ryan for bringing their enterprise down, the sibling group developed empathy for Ryan's condition and decided to be proactive and get him help. They encouraged him to enroll in a treatment program and altered his job to one that built on his skills but didn't require entertaining customers (events that often involved drinking). Ryan became able to function better, be healthier and achieve the metrics for success at work. This not only reduced conflict in the family business, but it also brought them closer as they agreed to work together to protect other family members from succumbing to their shared predilection to alcoholism.

Failure to communicate can lead to painful rifts in families. While some are understandable, they are painful nonetheless. For many families, issues that have kept siblings, cousins, and branches apart sometimes are often the result of miscommunications. Sometimes, the "perpetrator" doesn't even know what caused the rift. Two siblings, for example, who barely spoke to each other needed to make a joint decision about a shared family vacation home. During the course of the negotiations, Sandra talked about the horrible thing her sister Margaret had said about Sandra's husband that had caused her to decide to never speak to Margaret again.

Margaret was stunned – she said she had no recollection of ever having said such a thing and that if indeed she had, she was sure she hadn't meant it that way. Regardless, she was sorry for causing her sister such distress and was happy to finally know why Sandra had cut her out of her life. Simply by having that conversation and developing an understanding of what happened or may have happened, the sisters were able to move forward. They agreed that in the future if either of them was hurt by something the other said, they would check in to be sure they properly understood what they heard. By developing their communication skills, they hoped to prevent other such unfortunate misunderstandings in the future.

As family members improve their emotional intelligence, dispute resolution and communication skills, they are much more likely to become better partners in managing conflict.

Improving the Family Factor

Strengthening the Family Factor has a tremendous impact on the level of conflict in a family enterprise. As discussed in the previous chapter, a strong family bond is better able to leverage compromise and a commitment to change from stakeholders. Increasing the Family Factor is not an attempt to get family members to hug or even to like each other. Instead, if they have a robust shared history, they will have something to lose by exploding in conflict. Similarly, if they have a vision for being family in the future, they will have something to gain by keeping their conflict in check. And, if they can build trust, they might be able to consider making decisions outside their own individual interests and in the interests of others. The stronger the family bond, the greater ability they have to successfully manage conflict.

Adjusting Interdependence

Changing stakeholder roles in a family enterprise system in order to manage conflict should be undertaken with great care. Inexperienced advisors may view role changes as the simplest, most direct mechanism for managing conflict in a challenging family business conflict situation. However, due to the systemic nature of conflict in a family business, and the often unique importance that individual roles may have for stakeholders, simply adjusting roles, (i.e., interdependence) may actually be counterproductive; increasing rather than decreasing conflict.

Chapter 9 will discuss interdependence in great depth. When changes to individual stakeholder roles are considered with regard to their impact on the whole system and when these changes are explored, discussed and decided in a manner that avoids using power in a way that could be disrespected by the targets of that power, changing roles can help family enterprise systems move forward and away from conflict. Sometimes promotions, ownership transition and even removal from positions of power can be good for the system.

Summary

- There are five approaches that can be used to manage conflict – Dispute Resolution techniques, Releasing Blame, Development (Structural or Personal), increasing the Family Factor, and adjusting Interdependence.
- Dispute Resolution techniques include force (deciding/ voting, litigation, arbitration, coercion) and bargaining (negotiation, mediation, collaborative law, consensus building).
- Systemic, identity-based conflicts are not suited to force or bargaining, although simple dissension over power and money might respond to Dispute Resolution techniques.
- Releasing Blame refers to a process of forgiveness.
- Development approaches include Structural Development and Personal Development. These approaches attempt to grow the family and the system out of conflict through implementation of policies and procedures, articulation of job descriptions and accountability, coaching, and education.
- Increasing the Family Factor is the most effective way to lay the foundation for managing family conflict. While its goal is not to get family members to like one another better, increased family affinity is often a byproduct.
- Adjusting Interdependence can lessen conflict in the short term, but may create challenges in the longer term.
- *The Conflict Equation:*

$$C_t \propto \frac{ID \times DP \times (OG + IV + HI)}{FF \times (SD + PD + DR + RB)} + XF$$

Key

C_t = Conflict over Time	$\propto$ = is proportional to	ID = Interdependence
OG = Opposing Goals	IV = Incompatible Values	HI = Historical Impasse
DP = Disrespected Power	FF = Family Factor	XF = External Factors
SD = Structural Development	PD = Personal Development	DR = Dispute Resolution
RB = Releasing Blame		

Figure 7-2

Chapter 8

Applying *The Conflict Equation*

Problems that remain persistently insolvable should always be suspected as questions asked in the wrong way.

— Alan W. Watts

$$C_t \propto \frac{ID \times DP \times (OG + IV + HI)}{FF \times (SD + PD + DR + RB)} + XF$$

Key

C_t = Conflict over Time	$\propto$ = is proportional to	ID = Interdependence
OG = Opposing Goals	IV = Incompatible Values	HI = Historical Impasse
DP = Disrespected Power	FF = Family Factor	XF = External Factors
SD = Structural Development	PD = Personal Development	DR = Dispute Resolution
RB = Releasing Blame		

Figure 8-1

Now that we have explored the individual components that make up *The Conflict Equation*, it's time to put that equation to use. A key element of doing so is identifying a conflict manager. The conflict manager might be a stakeholder, an existing trusted advisor to a family, or a neutral third party called in to help when conflict arises. The concepts outlined in this book provide all individuals entrusted to serve as conflict manager with a deeper understanding of the situation they have been asked to address. This book also offers a powerful set of tools to help stakeholders manage conflict on an ongoing basis.

When the conflict manager is also a stakeholder involved in the conflict, it is important to understand how this might affect his or her stakeholder role and how being a stakeholder might impact his or her ability to be an effective conflict manager. A stakeholder is anyone in the family enterprise system who has a current or expected/future stake in the performance of the family enterprise – and, thus, the conflicts that surround the enterprise. This could include family members both in and out of the management of the company, family members who own stock in the business and those who don't, and those in line for an inheritance. Stakeholders can even include non-family managers and in-laws.

It is important that stakeholders wanting to use the methods described in this book understand that there are limits to how effective they can be in managing a conflict that they are part of. However, understanding the concepts described in this book will enable them to be as effective as possible in managing conflict from the inside. This book can help stakeholders better understand how their own behavior impacts the level of conflict in the system, and what they can do to pursue their interests more effectively while also reducing conflict. Armed with this information, and modeling more collaborative behavior, stakeholders can more effectively influence others to adopt behaviors that will be less conflictual, thus leading to solutions that are more reliable and that attend to the shared interests of all stakeholders.

The conflict manager might be formally identified as such by the key stakeholders. Or, the conflict manager may exist only as an archetype, a way for stakeholders to gauge their behavior against the concepts presented in this book. For example, a stakeholder group might ask: "How would a conflict manager evaluate what's going on and what might they suggest to remedy the situation?" Additionally, the conflict manager role may fall to a team of trusted advisors, each having their own area of specialization (law, psychology, business, etc.), but who all understand the concepts laid out in this book and who can work together to guide stakeholders in pursuit of their interests while keeping conflict in check. Or, the conflict manager might be a group of stakeholders using the concepts in this book to manage an existing conflict, or keep one from developing.

The Conflict Equation gives the conflict manager an understanding of the following three critical points:

- The relative level of, or potential for, conflict in a family business system;
- The components of conflict that are causing conflict (in relation to each other); and
- The ways in which the level of conflict can be managed.

It helps stakeholders and their advisors manage conflict by putting all the data together so they can develop robust and comprehensive strategies. To show how this works, let us first take stock of the equation we have built in the preceding chapters:

$$C_t \propto \frac{ID \times DP \times (OG + IV + HI)}{FF \times (SD + PD + DR + RB)} + XF$$

Key

C_t = Conflict over Time	$\propto$ = is proportional to	ID = Interdependence
OG = Opposing Goals	IV = Incompatible Values	HI = Historical Impasse
DP = Disrespected Power	FF = Family Factor	XF = External Factors
SD = Structural Development	PD = Personal Development	DR = Dispute Resolution
RB = Releasing Blame		

Figure 8-2

Conflict Component Review

Let's briefly review each of the components of *The Conflict Equation*.

C_t represents the level of **Conflict**, or the potential that exists for conflict. Its subscript "t" reminds us that conflict situations are not static and that each term in *The Conflict Equation* needs to be considered with regard to **Time**.

ID represents the level of **Interdependence** that exists in the system. The more interdependent stakeholders are in the family business system, the higher the potential for conflict. A family enterprise with complex ownership structures involving several family branches and generations, and where several family members including, perhaps, in-laws, work at the company may be more prone to conflict than a family with simpler ownership structures and fewer family employees at the firm.

Initially, we look at ID as a given, not as a variable. That is, we are not interested in reducing interdependence as a shortcut for managing conflict. Rather, we seek to manage conflict with the existing level of interdependence, if possible. In order to evaluate ID, the conflict manager must understand who is related to whom, which family members work at the company, which family members and key executives own stock, who are the trustees, who are the key advisors, and how these groups are expected to evolve over time. Based on this review, the conflict manager will make a judgment as to whether the family business has a high, low or moderate level of Interdependence, and how Interdependence might evolve to keep conflict at bay. This is where experience and judgment from working with many family businesses becomes important for any conflict manager.

DP represents the triggers for conflict: **Disrespected Power.** It is crucial to understand who holds power in the system and how each stakeholder uses the power he or she has. Power must be evaluated from the perspective of all types of power that was discussed in Chapter 5. Specifically, the conflict manager seeks to identify examples of where the use of power was disrespected in the past and how the use of power might be disrespected now and in the future.

OG represents the first of the underlying reasons for conflict: **Opposing Goals.** The conflict manager must be familiar enough with each stakeholder to understand their individual goals and to then determine how and with whom these goals are aligned, where they are different, and where they are in opposition to the goals of others.

IV represents the second of the underlying reasons for conflict: **Incompatible Values.** The conflict manager must be familiar enough with each stakeholder to understand all the relevant values that they hold. By relevant, we mean values that impact their role in the family business system, that drive the goals they may have identified, and that influence the relationships they have with other stakeholders. Remember, we are using the term "values" to cover many of the emotional and relationship issues that underlie conflict. "Incompatible Values," therefore, also considers the clash of personalities and beliefs as well as psychological dysfunction and addiction. The conflict manager must understand which values relate to the identity of each stakeholder, and which values a stakeholder might see as important, self-defining, and non-negotiable. The conflict manager must then be able to identify which of these values are aligned with others, which are different and, most importantly, which are incompatible with those of other stakeholders.

HI represents the third reason for conflict: **Historical Impasse.** The conflict manager must sift through family stories to discover which past events, perceived betrayals, and disagreements have become part of the fabric of discontent in the family, and which impact relationships and decision-making in the present.

FF represents the **Family Factor**. It cannot be overstated that this is the most influential variable in *The Conflict Equation*. As previously discussed, it is the answer to the question "Is the family bond strong enough to leverage compromise and a commitment to change?" The Family Factor may be stronger with some family members and weaker with others. But, we are interested in the aggregate. By understanding the building blocks of the Family Factor — shared history, trust and shared vision for being family in the future – the conflict manager can determine if the Family Factor is sufficient to help the family manage conflict together or if the Family Factor can be strengthened by building or rebuilding a shared history, developing a shared vision for being family in the future, or building trust (i.e., predictability).

SD represents **Structural Development** and it is the first of the conflict management approaches to consider. The conflict manager should first review all subsystems in the family business system – family, ownership, management, governance and advisory — to gauge how developed those structures are. These subsystems will be discussed in greater detail in the next chapter. From well-developed org-charts and job descriptions to recently reviewed estate plans and trust agreements, every subsystem needs to be evaluated to ensure that it is well-structured and that the structures in place are sufficient to enable conflict to be managed.

PD represents the second of the conflict management approaches: **Personal Development**. The conflict manager should be familiar enough with each stakeholder to assess whether each has appropriate skills and experience commensurate with their role in the family business system. Whether they are trustees, owners, managers, in-laws or serve any other role or combination of roles, people's skill set gaps need to be identified by the conflict manager. Each of these roles will be discussed in greater detail in the next chapter. In addition to specific, role-based skills, it is important to also assess the general communication, emotional intelligence, and conflict management skills of each stakeholder.

DR represents opportunities for **Dispute Resolution**. The conflict manager must identify individual, isolatable disputes that are not perceived as relating to the identity or survival of any stakeholder, and where traditional dispute resolution techniques might provide opportunities to clear the decks of these issues relatively quickly. The conflict manager must take care to ensure that the use of these techniques does not trigger additional conflict or render those issues the stuff of future Historical Impasse. Mediation, voting, consensus building, using legitimate authority to decide, or even the limited use of litigation might actually serve to rid the system of minor disputes which prove distracting to stakeholders who need to focus on more important threats to the family business system. Dispute resolution techniques might be considered for disputes over who holds power and how it is used, specific behaviors, opposing goals, and distribution of assets.

RB represents a process for forgiveness: **Releasing Blame**. It is specifically directed to resolving past disputes which have become, over time, Historical Impasses. The conflict manager must be skilled in facilitating a process for releasing blame. One such process, for example, was described in Chapter 7. Families who share a devotion to the same set of religious traditions may find that their faith speaks to the process of forgiveness. For this to be effective, however, all parties seeking a forgiveness process must subscribe to the same belief system.

XF represents a component of conflict not discussed since Chapter 2: **External Factors**. The conflict manager must understand the industry, economy, or competitive landscape enough to lead clients towards an awareness of the threats to the family business system that they do not directly control. Unexpected health challenges among family members, data breaches, robberies, and economic shifts in the family business industry are examples of external factors. The conflict manager must also have the perspective to inform stakeholders that conflict has arisen, in part, from factors that are outside the stakeholders' control.

Data Collection

Using *The Conflict Equation* begins with collecting the data. In the following chapters, we offer additional tools to help stakeholders and advisors collect the needed data to properly evaluate the family enterprise system. In this chapter, we show how *The Conflict Equation* provides a roadmap that identifies what data is relevant to understanding and managing conflict in the family business system. There are two primary ways to gather data: personal interviews and document analysis.

Personal Interviews

There is a significant benefit to having trained independent consultants facilitate personal interviews. Stakeholders who might be tempted to do this themselves must realize that they bring their own issues, roles, perspectives and biases into the interview process. This is especially problematic when stakeholders are in conflict. In such cases, the interview process itself could trigger conflict, as the interviewee may view the interviewer as having been given power (leadership of a conflict management effort, or ability to interpret the result of the interview process, for example) that they may not respect.

Once an interview process has been agreed to, it is important to cast the widest net possible regarding which stakeholders should be interviewed. As outside consultants, we generally embark on a two-stage interview process. An initial set of interviews with the obvious "key" stakeholders typically informs us about who in the larger constellation of stakeholders should be interviewed. Key stakeholders are those who are major shareholders, family leaders or important managers in the enterprise. An important trusted advisor might also be interviewed at this stage as well.

Three Groups of People to Interview

- Anyone with particular knowledge that we anticipate will be useful in better understanding each of the components of conflict outlined in *The Conflict Equation*. This includes trusted advisors to key stakeholders, trustees, and non-family key employees.
- Anyone who can influence or will be significantly affected by any potential outcome of the conflict management process. This often includes in-laws, retired grandparents, and children of college age.
- Anyone who might be offended by not being interviewed, and thus become unsupportive of the conflict management process.

The interview process is intended to be an open conversation, not a Q&A or a survey. Once a stakeholder is engaged in talking about the family business system, in his or her own words and according to his or her own priorities, the answers to the important questions will flow naturally. The conflict manager conducting the interview might occasionally guide the conversation to include some topics or detail important to the process that may not have been addressed by the stakeholder in open conversation.

The purpose of the interviews is to understand the business and family systems with regard to the components of conflict identified in *The Conflict Equation* (see list of interview objectives, below). As the conflict manager guides the discussion along each of the following paths, he or she should listen for how responses and stories relate to each of the twelve components of conflict outlined in *The Conflict Equation* and how those responses compare to those of other stakeholders. A listing of which components may be most relevant to each interview goal follows in parentheses. However, the conflict manager should be familiar enough with every component of conflict to listen for connections with any conflict component at all times during the interview process.

Interview Objectives

1. Understand who is related to whom, and how they are each related. (ID, FF, DP)
2. Understand which relationships are close, which are distant, and which are in conflict under stress. (FF, OG, IV, HI, DP)
3. Understand who owns stock in the business currently, who used to own stock and who may become an owner in the future. (ID, OG, IV, HI)
4. Understand how ownership is transitioned in the family business system and where voting control is held. (SD, OG, DP)
5. Understand who works in the family business currently, who worked there in the past, and who may work there in the future. Understand each role and the competency that each stakeholder brings to their role in the business. (ID, SD, PD, OG, IV)
6. Understand how family is selected for opportunities to work in the company. (SD, OG, IV, HI)
7. Understand when in time certain key events took place, or when they are anticipated to take place in the future. (FF, HI)

8. Understand each individual's goals, values and histories as they relate to each other and the family business system. (OG, IV, HI, FF)
9. Understand the industry, the competitive environment, the technology and the economic factors that impact the business and may present threats in the future. (XF)
10. Understand the general health and education levels and skill sets of family members. (XF, PD)

As the conflict manager becomes more familiar with *The Conflict Equation*, and each of its component terms, the interview process will appear seamless and will provide most of the information needed to understand and manage conflict in the family business system. Follow-up interviews are often very useful with the key stakeholder group to ensure that nothing is missed and that no errors were made regarding the data collected.

Document Analysis

In addition to personal interviews, much of the information needed to understand and manage conflict in the family business system is contained in the myriad of documents that relate to the company, its ownership, the estate plan, and the management of family wealth. We provide here a list of common documents that should be reviewed. By no means is this list exhaustive. Depending on the issues at hand, there may be additional contracts and agreements, deeds, and other documents that also need to be reviewed.

Documents to Review

1. Corporate Bylaws and Governance Documents
2. Buy-Sell and Stock Restriction Agreements
3. Schedule of Stock Ownership
4. Company Org Chart, including Board of Directors
5. Job Descriptions and Employment Contracts
6. Company Financials (5 years) and Company Valuation
7. Company Employee Manual
8. Policy Statements, including: Family Employment, Family Employee Review and Compensation
9. Company Mission/Vision/Values Statement
10. Estate Plans and Trust Documents
11. Company Strategic Plan and SWOT Analysis
12. Family Genogram, dates for key family events (births, deaths, marriages, etc.)

13. Family Constitution/Mission/Value Statements
14. Investment Portfolios for Key Stakeholders (as appropriate)
15. Philanthropic Entity Information
16. Standard Lease Agreements
17. Schedule of Lease Maturity and Vacancies
18. Appraisals
19. Mortgage Documents
20. Broker, Supplier, Vendor, and Customer Contracts

Families are unlikely to have all these documents available and, even if they exist, they may not be current or relevant. The mere fact that they may not have every document listed above does not mean that there is a need to develop each document. To the extent that the enterprise has the documentation, policies, and agreements it needs to conduct business and manage relationships with each stakeholder group without conflict, the business would be considered as having an appropriate level of structural development. When documentation is absent, obsolete or incomplete, consider whether creating or updating any document would address a specific deficiency, need, or conflict that exists now or that may exist in the future. Creating documents without a well-articulated purpose may prove counterproductive, as even the most well-intentioned change may work against the perceived interests of some of the stakeholders.

Like the interview process, document analysis is intended to provide data on the components of *The Conflict Equation*. Document analysis is likely to provide information regarding who in the system holds legitimate authority (power) and how stakeholders are connected to each other through ownership, agreement and hierarchy. Document analysis might also help identify and explain Historical Impasses and Opposing Goals related to wealth and power. The point is that we never know what we will find during the data collection process. Being familiar with the components of *The Conflict Equation* will guide the process, help conflict managers look for needed information, and make sure that important data is not missed.

While sufficient data is needed to understand the magnitude of each of the components in the equation, the data itself does not help manage conflict. Instead, by using the data to understand the relative magnitude of each of the components in *The Conflict Equation*, the conflict manager learns how the family business system works and where the tensions lie. Using the tools presented in this book to organize the data allows a conflict manager to more easily sketch a picture of the family system and begin to understand how individuals function within the context of the systems in which they operate. By combining the data with professional knowledge, experience, and judgment, the conflict manager can develop strategies to grow the family enterprise system out of active conflict, or get it unstuck.

Data Analysis Charts

Once all the relevant data has been collected, it is useful to summarize the data in a workable format. For example, the conflict manager may have spoken to all the relevant stakeholders, reviewed all the relevant documentation, and have notebooks full of information. The next task for the conflict manager is to determine, from this data, all the reasons and triggers (both active and potential) for conflict in all parts of the system, and among all stakeholders, that exist. The conflict manager must also have a sense for the strength of the Family Factor, how the stakeholders are connected to each other (i.e., Interdependence), how each part of the family business system operates, how it is structured, what policies and agreements are in place, and how it interacts with the outside world.

Obviously, there is a lot of data to collect and analyze. *The Conflict Equation*, supported by the tools described in this book, is an organizing framework that makes this process manageable, consistent and thorough.

One particularly useful way to visually present this information is to create a series of charts set up with each term that contributes to conflict on the left side of the chart, with the associated approaches for its management on the right side of the chart.

For example, reading through interview notes and document summaries may have helped the conflict manager identify several of the important goals for each key stakeholder. Reviewing these to identify which goals among the group are in opposition is the purpose of this stage of analysis. Doing the same to determine where relevant values are incompatible, and identifying what historical impasses exist, will help identify and organize all the underlying reasons for conflict. The "Opposing Goals" chart would list each identified opposing goal on the left; ideas for managing each of those items, that are consistent with the type of approach that is effective in managing Opposing Goals, would appear on the right.

Reviewing the notes and documents will also help the conflict manager identify where power is held in the system, where positions of power are disrespected, and where the use of power is disrespected in the system. All these instances of disrespected power, therefore, would be listed in a chart for Disrespected Power. The strength of the family bond, as defined by each of the three components that make up the Family Factor, would also be listed in its respective chart. Building out individual charts for each component of conflict is a useful strategy for identifying options for managing conflict.

Finally, a SWOT (Strengths, Weaknesses, Opportunities and Threats) analysis (explored more thoroughly in Chapter 9) may identify external opportunities and threats that are impacting the business, or that could in the future. It is important to include threats and opportunities to the enterprise coming from family dynamics and structure. These are often overlooked in a traditional SWOT analysis for a business, but they are essential for analyzing family businesses. Note that the analysis of strengths and weaknesses will identify existing levels of both structural and personal development impacting the business system. A separate SWOT analysis can be done for the family and must include opportunities and threats coming from the business.

Once all the information has been compiled and analyzed, the conflict manager has:

- determined the reasons and triggers for conflict,
- gauged the ability of family members to compromise or change for the sake of family cohesiveness,
- considered the impact of outside forces,
- understood the existing level of structural and personal development as it relates to each system, and
- learned how each stakeholder is interdependent within the enterprise system.

The conflict manager is now ready to design a conflict management plan.

Developing a Conflict Management Plan

As we have said often throughout this book, *The Conflict Equation* does not seek to quantitatively measure conflict or to generate any numbers. Rather, it allows stakeholders to gauge the relative level of conflict and to see how changes to the system serve to increase or decrease conflict. Also, keep in mind that we are using a very expansive definition of conflict that includes situations when families are stuck. We are not only looking at when families are engaged in active fighting. Passive conflict can be just as destructive over time to a family enterprise. When families are stuck, they delay making important decisions for fear of conflicts that may ensue; opportunities are squandered, competitive pressures mount, and conflict builds up to its inevitable breaking point.

> *The Conflict Equation* does not seek to quantitatively measure conflict or to generate any numbers. Rather, it allows stakeholders to gauge the relative level of conflict and see how changes to the system serve to increase or decrease conflict.

After all the data is analyzed, the conflict manager can develop a plan by creating specific strategies to address each component of conflict within each specific conflict management approach (i.e., dispute resolution techniques, development opportunities, and opportunities for releasing blame).

Start with What Triggers Active Conflict

The most urgent issue when family business stakeholders are in active conflict is to try to stop additional conflict from being triggered, thus escalating the problems already at issue. In order to do this, we look to Disrespected Power.

By reviewing who holds power, how power is used, and where the use of power is being disrespected, we can begin to consider what changes we may suggest to reduce the use of Disrespected Power. Power, and behavior around the use of power, responds to many of the conflict management approaches that we have discussed.

> *The Conflict Equation* doesn't dictate specific solutions, but it provides an organizing structure to think through approaches that might be beneficial – and, it helps identify approaches that cannot be effective, so they can be avoided.

Although power responds to bargaining and force, the use of power in a family business is most likely a systemic characteristic and not an isolated event or incident. Temporary or limited cessations of the use of power may be negotiated to buy time. Trying to use force or bargaining to instill a permanent change in the power balance at the office, or to make lasting change in the behavior of the person wielding power at the outset of this process before all stakeholders are invested in the more comprehensive process, will likely not be effective, and may end up triggering additional conflict.

If the use of force is a current issue, Structural Development and Personal Development (rather than Releasing Blame) would be the most effective means to provide long-term, reliable change to the balance of power and to how power is used. Perhaps there are ambiguous rules and a lack of clarity regarding how power is distributed in the family business system that could be addressed through developing better documents and policy. Perhaps there are skill set gaps in leadership that can be reduced through personal coaching.

There is no single best way to address each type of issue. Every family is unique; some members may gravitate to one solution while others would respond better to something different. An experienced conflict manager could educate stakeholders in how other family businesses have solved similar problems. While this may provide interesting perspective and facilitate good brainstorming, what has worked for similar families in the past won't necessarily apply to every family. Perhaps an independent board was created so there was recourse when an executive was perceived by some to overstep his or her authority. Maybe the incident has exposed a problem of insufficiently detailed job descriptions – leaving issues of power ambiguous. Maybe by identifying the problem as one of power distribution, the family could devise creative solutions such as rotating authority for a decision-making role among branches every quarter or every year. These would be structural approaches to managing power balance in the system.

It may also be that a problem lies with the perception that the use of power is somehow wrong and that conflict is being triggered inappropriately. That is, if the target of that power is operating under false assumptions about the illegitimacy of that power and how it is being used, conflict may be triggered when it shouldn't. Educating stakeholders about shareholder rights, duty of loyalty, and other areas of business that involve power are examples of how Personal Development can be extremely effective.

The point is that regardless of the particular situation, *The Conflict Equation* will lead stakeholders and their advisors to the categories of solutions that can be effective for each component of conflict they encounter.

By deconstructing conflict in this way, its causes can be identified as specific components of *The Conflict Equation* and strategies can be developed to manage those conflicts. *The Conflict Equation* doesn't dictate specific solutions, but it provides an organizing structure in which to think through approaches that might be beneficial – and, it identifies approaches that cannot be effective, so they can be avoided.

Reduce the Reasons for Conflict

If the underlying reasons for conflict can be systematically identified and reduced, the potential for active conflict will also be reduced.

Addressing Opposing Goals

Goals are negotiable. They also respond to development. Conflict analysis may identify that stakeholders in the family business system have goals that are in opposition to each other. These opposing goals may be extremely important and self-defining for each stakeholder.

For example, two stakeholders may each fervently believe that they should be the sole leader of the enterprise – and, that it would mean ruin for the family and its business, if the other should prevail. Moreover, each of these stakeholders has their own constituencies of support. One's spouse may be extremely outspoken about her husband's qualifications for the top slot, and equally outspoken about his cousin's incompetence. That cousin, who also eyes the top slot, may be supported by employees who wield significant power in the system. In a family business, conflict is systemic and rarely involves just the individuals at the heart of the conflict or individual issues in isolation.

Recognizing that the opposing goals held by the cousins are part of a larger system of conflict informs us that every step of the conflict management process must be measured and must consider the system as a whole. Even though *The Conflict Equation* may lead us to consider solutions from development and bargaining, we must always consider the impact of these solutions on the broader system – both now and in the future. *The Conflict Equation* provides the framework to do exactly this.

Depending on the particular characteristics and circumstances of the family enterprise system, options and recommendations can be developed. For example, a Structural Development approach to managing the cousins' opposing goals in the example cited above might consider asking a task force to develop a set of guidelines and requirements for succession to the top slot. Institutionalizing the succession process would serve to de-personalize the selection. An independent board or search committee might be developed to manage this process in a way that didn't risk important family relationships.

A Personal Development approach, including a comprehensive 360-degree review process, might provide for training and coaching to be offered to both stakeholders so that a clear leader might emerge. Or, by having each contender better understand each other's point of view, and be educated about the risks and benefits of each other's proposed strategy for the company, perhaps consensus might emerge.

Dispute resolution techniques that seek to expand choices might identify opportunities for sharing leadership or getting the battling cousins to agree together on the choice of an outside leader.

Every situation will be different and each will generate a different set of possible solutions. The power of *The Conflict Equation* is that it provides a framework for understanding and evaluating potential solutions based on which approaches are appropriate for each source of conflict, and which should be avoided.

Addressing Incompatible Values

Incompatible Values are not negotiable, nor can changes in any individual's value system be forced. Values and beliefs only respond to development. Risk tolerance, for example, is a value that is held by stakeholders in varied ways. Consider the case of two sisters with equal ownership and leadership positions in the company they inherited who must make joint decisions on corporate strategy. Their decisions will dictate investments to be made, their ability to distribute income, and whom they chose to hire. One sister wants the company to remain small and stable, to focus on quality, and to support her current lifestyle. The other wants to borrow or raise capital to expand nationally, build equity, and perhaps sell to a larger brand. Their differences in risk tolerance drive many of the goals they each have for themselves and for the business. If they can find a way to embrace each other's relationship with risk, and overcome their incompatible attitudes towards risk, they will be able to find alignment in decision-making.

Perhaps one sister's discomfort with risk stems from a lack of understanding of corporate finance and inexperience with growth-stage companies. Education (i.e., Personal Development) may go a long way to helping her overcome her resistance to risk. Her sister may seek to better understand why there is such a difference in their risk tolerance. She may be led, through coaching or psychology, to develop more empathy for her sister and to better understand her sister's financial circumstances that cause her to be less risk-tolerant. Consensus, forged from increased empathy and understanding, might be possible.

While one can't bargain with one's values, accommodation can be developed through structure (aka Structural Development). Perhaps the less risk-tolerant sister can be protected from the downside of expansion risks through agreements, like stock put options or a sum of money set aside in escrow for her if the strategy fails.

Although values cannot be negotiated, there are plenty of ways, through Structural and Personal Development, to accommodate seemingly Incompatible Values and for those values to evolve through education and experience. Building empathy and understanding for stakeholder values can overcome Incompatible Values and strengthen the family bond.

Addressing Historical Impasse

The only approach for addressing Historical Impasse is a process for releasing blame, or forgiving. As described in Chapter 7, a forgiveness process offers several choices, including refusing to forgive. Often, families are highly committed to their historical narrative. To them, anecdotes have become fact, and real or perceived injustices were as they were told and, for the most part, intentional. Rejecting the historic family narrative, or at least reframing it within the context of other perspectives, is difficult. But, if it can be done, a forgiveness process may be able to take hold.

Sometimes recompense, apology, acknowledgement of wrong-doing or mistake, and promises not to recommit an offense are required to release blame. Each of these acts requires the coop-eration and sincere involvement of the perceived transgressor. In some cases, a level of acceptance of the situation can be achieved by one party alone, without the involvement of the other party. Through acceptance, blame may be able to be released.

Any pragmatic approach for releasing blame will have at its core a process of evaluating one's own contribution to an im-passe. Every result of a forgiveness process must provide an ex-pectation that a transgression will not be repeated. Sometimes, while there is no true reconciliation, just acknowledging the anger and letting each party have an opportunity to vent and explain will enable stakeholders to move forward by agreeing to disagree.

Forgiveness is a core concept in every religion and each has a forgiveness process within its teaching and tradition. When stakeholders in conflict over Historical Impasse also share a deep commitment to the same religious tradition, they may find a path to genuine forgiveness through their faith. When they don't share each other's faith, however, any attempt to push one's faith-based process for forgiveness will fail and possibly generate additional instances of Incompatible Values.

Improve the Family Factor

As a multiplier in the denominator, no matter what compo-nent of conflict is wreaking havoc in the family business system, improving the Family Factor is the one effort that amplifies every approach to managing conflict. Improving the Family Factor helps stakeholders agree to compromise, and commit to making important personal and structural changes in order to achieve an outcome that supports family harmony.

> No matter what component of conflict is wreaking havoc in the family business system, im-proving the Family Factor is the one effort that amplifies every approach to managing conflict.

In Chapter 6 we deconstructed the Family Factor into its component parts: shared history, trust, and shared vision for being family in the future. Build-ing the Family Factor begins with the shared understanding that even if the family's goal is not to be close in the future, it is important to build the Family Factor to manage current conflict. In addition, family members do not have to like each other to have a strong Family Factor.

Strengthening Shared History

As we have said, when families have a deep, shared history with each other, they have something to lose if they are unable to manage conflict well. Some families have few shared memories or histories together. Family members, or entire family branches, may have moved out of the homestead generations ago and get together only infrequently. Other families may be geographically close, but worlds apart emotionally, with few shared experiences among them. Still other families may have developed deep resentments over the years and have purposefully stayed distant. These families are at a disadvantage when it comes to resiliency in the face of conflict – and some level of conflict in a family enterprise system is inevitable.

Strengthening shared history begins by creating a shared narrative of the family's history. There may not be many shared stories, but there are individual stories for each stakeholder. Sharing these individual stories brings families together. Facebook pages, websites, and retreats are excellent ways to begin building a shared history.

In addition, a cottage industry has developed around creating family narratives in book or video formats. Family biographies and documentaries can be sourced from many authors and producers who specialize in working with families and family businesses to tell their stories. Having such a resource can serve to recast the family history in a positive light that individual family members can be proud of. Again, when family members are connected to each other through meaningful shared experience, or shared history, they have something to lose if they allow conflict to overwhelm them.

For families that have deep historical resentments, a process of releasing blame, or forgiveness, might be the starting point. Lessons learned from a history of separateness may have greater meaning when family relationships are restored and those lessons become a shared history.

Building a Shared Vision for Being Family in the Future

When family members believe that staying connected as family is important to their future, the family has something to gain by managing conflict with each other effectively. Exploring the potential benefits of staying connected as a family can help build the Family Factor and make the family more resilient to conflict. Staying together as family isn't always easy. It takes effort and can be risky. There often has to be a purpose behind making the effort.

Such purpose is evidenced when families are locked into legacy agreements for sharing assets or connected by opportunities for managing a family business together. These families can buy some insurance against the risks of extreme conflict by ensuring that family members continue to know each other and share experiences together. A shared belief that close, engaged family relationships support good working relationships and shared ownership will give stakeholders a purpose for staying connected and involved in each other's lives.

Creating structural opportunities for family members to stay connected and share experiences despite time, distance, and diminishing blood ties is key to maintaining a shared vision of being family for the future. Annual retreats, holiday meals, educational programs relating to the family business, and communication platforms such as newsletters and blogs can help build that vision. These structures provide relevant education and enjoyable shared experience that can be the glue that holds family together. Family banks and scholarships can provide tangible, financial benefits for keeping family intact for the long term.

Shared philanthropy can serve a powerful purpose: keeping families connected and practiced in making decisions together. What makes shared philanthropy especially useful is that, properly administered, there are few opportunities for self-interest to cloud the work, and the decision-making focuses on ways "to do good" in society. That said, shared philanthropy can be difficult when family members are geographically dispersed and somewhat disconnected. Often, individuals prefer to give locally, where their generosity can be acknowledged and where they can see the impact of their generosity. When family is geographically dispersed, finding alignment on the targets of their shared philanthropy may prove difficult. In addition, sharing philanthropy among different generations can be difficult because generational values may be significantly different, leading to different philanthropic interests.

Another incentive for building a shared vision for being family relates to avoiding a pattern of cutoffs (we discuss this in greater detail in Chapter 10). When families view family as disposable when conflict looms, and they cut family members out of their lives in anger, they teach that lesson to younger generations and generations not yet born. These future generations are then more likely to experience cutoffs in their families when the inevitable conflict strikes.

Again, when stakeholders share the vision of being a strong, connected family in the future, they have something to gain if they are able to manage conflict together. Thus when there is a strong, shared vision for being family in the future, there is more energy for achieving compromise and working towards needed change.

Building Trust

As discussed in Chapter 7, the type of trust that is pertinent in building the Family Factor is trust that comes from family members knowing each other well and being able to predict how each will react when power is used in the system. It is not the kind of trust that derives from the assumption that individuals have each other's best interests at heart. People can trust each other without necessarily liking each other or having the same goals and values.

When stakeholders know each other well and have sufficient ability to predict the broad outline of each other's responses to change, family members can make measured decisions to forward their interests with a reasonable certainty about how those decisions will impact others, and the family business system at large. It is this concern about the larger system of family that is important. For example, a stakeholder may not care much for his cousin and may not have her best interests at heart. However, by knowing what her likely reaction to a decision might be, that stakeholder will be better able to consider the best interests of the family system in making that decision, because he can predict the impact of his cousin's reaction to that decision. As a result of this "trust," conflict can be anticipated and managed, allowing the family enterprise system to move forward.

A family constitution or a well-articulated set of family values can support trust in a family. If there are rules and expectations set forth for how family will treat each other and what is important to the family – and if these evolve and have continual buy-in as the family evolves – trust can flourish. Just as our laws, our constitution, and our traditions in society allow trust to build in our communities, so too will such documentation support trust in a family.

The processes and structures mentioned above for building shared history and a shared vision of being family in the future also help build trust because family members learn more about each other through those efforts. The better they know each other, the more predictability is built into the system and, therefore, the better able individuals are to make decisions to further the family enterprise system – beyond their own personal interests.

Consider External Factors

The conflict manager must be knowledgeable enough about the external environment in which the family exists to help family members gain perspective on how their family and its enterprise are impacted by outside events that they can't control. Families sometimes need reminding that when the economy contracts and cash dries up, or when illness and misfortune hit, it is natural for stress and tensions to rise. Reframing a stressful situation to identify things that were external and beyond stakeholder control can help reduce finger-pointing and blame.

For example, a third-generation life-sciences company was hard-hit by the US government's sequester of research funding. This raised tensions within the executive team, the family members on that team, and the board members. Yet, the sequester was an external factor and thus no one's fault. All they could do was to work together to craft an enterprise-level response to the unfortunate situation. Routinely reminding each other that the sequester was out of their control helped the business, board and family teams stay aligned and effective.

Consider Adjusting Interdependence

At the beginning of this book, we identified that conflict can be reduced simply by reducing the Interdependence among stakeholders in the system. Clearly, one way to manage conflict in a family business is to take family members out of the business and the business out of the family. This is too often the advice coming from advisors whose interests are driven by an M&A transaction, advisors who are being judged by the singular business metric of top-line or bottom-line growth, advisors who are being judged by the singular metric of family harmony, and advisors who have thrown up their hands in despair in the face of extreme and intractable family business conflict.

Sometimes, however, individuals simply cannot work or own together, despite all the efforts discussed in this book. In these cases, reducing Interdependence might be considered. Siloing management functions within the business, restructuring the business into separate autonomous divisions, buying out branches, eliminating family employment, or selling the entire enterprise and having family members go their separate ways are all ways to accomplish this. There is nothing wrong with any of these choices, although they all will have significant ramifications over time that must be managed.

Within a family business, it is possible that leaders may have opposing visions of what they are trying to accomplish. If those disparate visions cannot be accommodated in some manner, there is a strong argument for separation. A wonderful movie that explores exactly this situation in a fun and realistic manner is the 1996 film *Big Night*, starring Stanley Tucci, Tony Shalhoub, and others. At its core is a story of two brothers trying to run a business together, each with a completely different definition of what "success" in that enterprise looks like. The film tells the story of how they balance being family while struggling with how to work together with their competing visions.

Adjusting Interdependence does not necessarily mean reducing Interdependence. Consider the case of "sticky-baton-syndrome." In family business systems, it often happens that departing leaders delay their departure, holding off passing the baton of leadership to the next generation. It is also not uncommon that this can create significant conflict. Leadership succession is a core challenge in adjusting Interdependence among stakeholders. Reframing leadership succession in this larger perspective, and seeing the process through the lens of conflict management, can help identify new ideas for facilitating such difficult change.

Adjusting Interdependence should be a consensus process. If it is done unilaterally, without the consent of all those affected, it can be seen as the use of Disrespected Power, and thus trigger even more conflict. In conflictual situations, it may be tempting for a stakeholder to reduce Interdependence by firing, disinheriting, ignoring or diverting corporate opportunity. Each of these is fraught with the likelihood of increased conflict (including lawsuits) in a family enterprise. When any stakeholder thinks a reduction of Interdependence would be helpful to the business or to family relationships, they need to be mindful of the existing interdependent structures and relationships involved. Transparency and consensus-building can make the reduction of Interdependence a positive for the family enterprise when other avenues for managing conflict have proven ineffective.

The Essential Role of the Conflict Manager

The Conflict Equation provides a roadmap for collecting and analyzing the data needed to develop approaches for managing the particular components of conflict that have been identified in the assessment process. The Deconstructing Conflict process described in this book helps identify which conflict management approaches are applicable for each component of conflict, but it does not dictate specific approaches, methods or techniques. The approach chosen depends upon the skill and experience of the conflict manager, the constellation of issues at play, the level of organization and "professionalization" of the family enterprise system, and the Family Factor.

The main responsibility of the conflict manager is to help the stakeholders, as a group, explore and understand the array of options that they can pursue to manage conflict, and their likely effects on the entire system. *The Conflict Equation* shows the components of conflict in relation to each other and how change in one component may positively impact other components, but might risk doing damage elsewhere in the system. It allows the conflict manager to evaluate how specific changes to the system will impact the overall level of conflict in the system.

A conflict manager needs to understand dispute resolution theory and technique and either be skilled in negotiation and facilitation or able to identify when outside specialists are needed. He or she needs to understand family systems and business, and be current in best practices and theory concerning family business and family wealth. Finally, the conflict manager needs to understand enough about corporate law, estate law, investment management, leadership development and the particular industry that the family is involved with, to either provide needed assistance or know when outside specialists are needed.

Above all, a conflict manager must understand the specific nature of conflict in families over wealth, power and business. This book is a guide for the process, but anyone considering the role of a conflict manager for a family enterprise should not underestimate the broad experience and skill sets required.

Summary

- The conflict manager who uses *The Conflict Equation* methodology should be a neutral advisor skilled in both business management and family systems.
- The conflict manager must collect a lot of data relevant to all aspects of the family enterprise system.
- The conflict manager gathers information through interviews and document analysis. Using specific tools, information can be categorized into the components of conflict, providing an objective view of the situation in the context of *The Conflict Equation*.
- A plan can be developed by identifying which approaches to managing conflict are needed to address the components of conflict at play in the situation.
- A plan of action may include limiting the use of Disrespected Power, reducing the Reasons for conflict, improving the Family Factor, evaluating and strategically addressing External Factors, and possibly adjusting the level of Interdependence in the system.
- The conflict manager plays a critical role in understanding and providing options for managing ongoing, systemic conflict.
- *The Conflict Equation*:

$$C_t \propto \frac{ID \times DP \times (OG + IV + HI)}{FF \times (SD + PD + DR + RB)} + XF$$

Key

C_t = Conflict over Time	$\propto$ = is proportional to	ID = Interdependence
OG = Opposing Goals	IV = Incompatible Values	HI = Historical Impasse
DP = Disrespected Power	FF = Family Factor	XF = External Factors
SD = Structural Development	PD = Personal Development	DR = Dispute Resolution
RB = Releasing Blame		

Figure 8-3

Chapter 9

Interdependence: The Structure of the Family Enterprise System

Never cut what you can untie.
— Robert Frost

All family business systems are unique, defined by the people involved, the roles they play and the rules that connect them. In this chapter, we take a closer look at stakeholder roles and introduce The Stakeholder Map, a graphic tool designed to detail interdependence among all stakeholders in the family business system.

We also introduce several other tools that help the conflict manager analyze the family business system from several different perspectives. From using the tools described in this chapter, a clear picture of the family business system emerges. Completing the tools and laying them out side-by-side presents an objective picture of the family relationships, the level of interdependence, and the enterprise structure in a way that shows specifically where support and change are needed.

> Family businesses are made up of many stakeholders with overlapping roles and responsibilities – high levels of stakeholder interdependence are built in. Because these interdependent roles involve issues of identity, wealth and power, conflict is virtually impossible to avoid.

As explained earlier, conflict cannot exist when there is zero interdependence among stakeholders. Family enterprise, however, is made up of many stakeholders with overlapping roles and responsibilities. Because these interdependent roles involve issues of identity, wealth, and power, conflict is virtually impossible to avoid. When conflict occurs in these systems, it can be extreme and seem intractable. Understanding and managing this interdependence, therefore, is a crucial step in the conflict management process.

The first step to managing interdependence in a family enterprise system is to understand precisely how family members are interconnected among each other, with their enterprise, and with the outside world. It is only with a thorough understanding of each specific subsystem in which family members operate that stakeholders can begin to manage that interdependence and, therefore, begin to manage conflict.

In this chapter, we present five tools that will help stakeholders and their advisors gain the perspective regarding stakeholder interdependence that is needed to apply *The Conflict Equation* and manage conflict.

The **genogram** is a tool developed by psychologists studying family systems. It is essentially a family tree with extra information added to it, in a particular format that is extremely useful for understanding the structure of families and how individuals relate to each other. It also can be a very useful database for stakeholder information.

The corporate **org-chart** is a common tool illustrating how a business is organized and where authority resides. The typical org-chart can be adapted to provide useful information for family business analysis.

A **document checklist** identifies which management and ownership transition plans are in place to deal with circumstances or crises that may arise.

A **SWOT (Strengths, Weaknesses, Opportunities, and Threats) analysis** identifies what is going well and what needs attention from a competitive strategy perspective. This analysis considers the strengths and weaknesses of the business and the opportunities and threats from all subsystems (including the family) that impact the enterprise. A separate SWOT analysis of the family system should also include opportunities and threats from its enterprise.

Finally, we describe the **Stakeholder Map**, a powerful tool that shows all the overlapping stakeholder roles that serve to make up the entire family business system. It is a single sheet of paper that shows graphically which subsystems each stakeholder participates in directly. It also can show movement, or potential movement, of stakeholders to additional or alternative constituent subsystems.

Understanding the Family Structure: The Genogram

Organized by generation and birth order within each family branch, the genogram shows who is related to whom, as well as how each stakeholder is emotionally connected to each other stakeholder. Various conventions have been developed to make genograms a widely applicable tool. For example, oldest siblings appear on the left and younger siblings appear on the right in descending age order. Males are depicted as squares and females as circles. There are many other conventions indicating how divorces, subsequent marriages, congenital health issues, and other characteristics are recorded. A complete tutorial is beyond the scope of this book, but we encourage readers to explore genograms for themselves.

The genogram was developed and popularized by Monica McGoldrick and Randy Gerson in 1985 and has become an essential tool for psychologists interested in studying family systems. It can, however, be an extremely useful tool for the conflict manager. The genogram looks like a family tree, but with much more information. In addition to showing who is related to whom, it shows birth order, gender, dates of birth and death, and can also display educational, professional and/or medical and psychological characteristics of each family member. It can also display emotional relationships between and among all family members, helping users to identify problematic relationships and family factions.

Genograms are particularly useful in helping stakeholders and their advisors grasp the complexity of large families and to keep track of who is in which branch, which relationships are strong, which are distant, which are in conflict, and which may be completely isolated from the rest of the family.

The genogram also helps the conflict manager identify structural issues in the family that impact many of the components of conflict we have already discussed in this book. For example, large multigenerational families may have significant age disparities within generations. Some branches may have many more children than others. Together, these structural issues may have a dramatic impact on the distribution of wealth or ownership in the family enterprise. Having a graphical representation of this information helps the conflict manager understand and keep track of it, and can sometimes be a way to help stakeholders gain valuable perspective about their families.

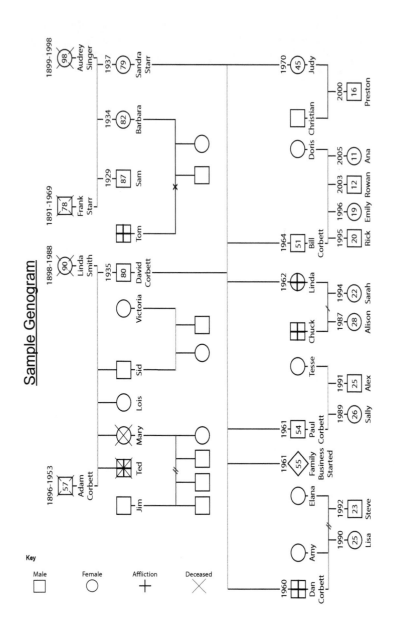

Figure 9-1   Sample Genogram

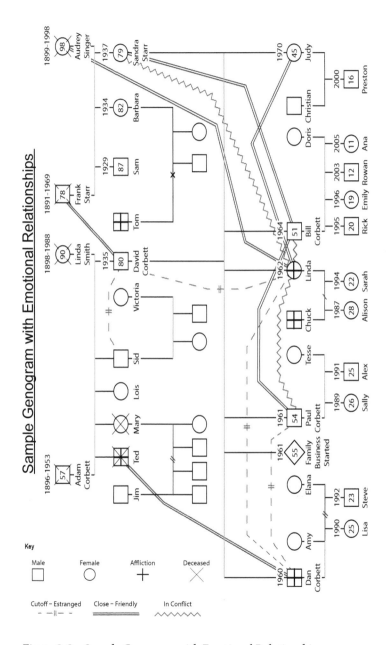

Figure 9-2   Sample Genogram with Emotional Relationships

A sample genogram of four generations of a family is shown in Figure 9-1, without the emotional relationship overlay, and in Figure 9-2, with the emotional relationship overlay. Generation 1, or G1, is at the top and Generation 4, or G4, is at the bottom. Notice how much important information about the family is contained in just these two images. One branch of a G3 sibling group is expanded in the genogram, as these were the siblings who owned and worked together in the family enterprise started by their parents.

Figure 9-1 shows us that the parents of the siblings in question were both the youngest in their families of origin. The dark crosses in some of the boxes indicate an affliction that impacted several members of this family. In this case, the affliction was alcoholism and it appears to be a shared predilection in the family. The lighter x's indicate that the person is deceased, and birth year and/or age is shown. The genogram also shows that one family has only one child, while another has four children. This tells us to be on the lookout for wealth disparity conflicts when the costs of education become relevant, and in the G4 when inheritance issues arise. The genogram shows the "birth" of the family business in 1961, just after the birth of the first of the siblings in this family.

Figure 9-2 shows the same constellation of people, but with the emotional relationship information overlaid. We can see that some siblings have great relationships with each other, while others have highly antagonistic relationships. We can also gain some insight into how older generations have been pulled into the factions and alliances in the sibling relationships. Of particular importance is that it shows that the father and his brother were cut off from each other (presumably due to unresolved conflict) and that this pattern of cutoff behavior continues in the next generation.

Gathering the "hard data" — the facts and figures that describe a family — is a relatively straightforward process. Such information as family hierarchy, significant dates, education, profession, afflictions, etc., can easily be supplied by family members themselves. Alternatively, a family member or consultant can be chosen to initiate an interview process to gather the pertinent "hard data." Genograms can be simple "back of the napkin" sketches or more elaborate computer databases that offer more detailed graphical information.

Gathering the "soft data" regarding the social and emotional relationships that exist between family members can be highly subjective and its collection is best facilitated by a consultant trained in family systems analysis, serving as an independent party. In order to accumulate the best possible data, the process should be confidential and/or anonymous. Not only can the genogramming process get an individual stakeholder to articulate goals, values, and problems with or between other stakeholders (and with the business entity itself), but it can also help stakeholders begin to think about their family as a system. A skillful conflict manager will be able to tease out information regarding what being "family" means to each stakeholder. Developing a basic genogram provides the conflict manager with a roadmap of whom else to interview in greater depth, both within the family and, in many cases, outside the family, because the process prompts deep conversation about the family and its enterprise.

The completed genogram provides a useful single-page summary of the family system. Along with interview notes, the conflict manager should have a thorough understanding of the particular family's system, including its structure, rules, values and purpose, as well as individual family members' histories, the status of their relationships with each other, and some insight into their concerns and motivations – as individuals and family groups.

While family members enjoy looking at their genogram, that is not why the conflict manager needs to create it. Rather, genograms can provide invaluable information for the conflict manager. For example, as we discussed in Chapter 6 in the context of the Family Factor, shared history is very relevant to the family bond. Accordingly, when we see that two siblings are fifteen years apart in age, we learn that although they grew up in the same household with the same parents, they may have been raised in very different circumstances, may barely know each other, and may have very little shared experience. We would wonder whether these siblings shared the same values and consider each other close. In some families a wide age discrepancy may indeed imply a low Family Factor. Other families may have been able to forge close sibling relationships and a strong family identity despite significant age disparity among the sibling (or cousin) group.

Birth order is another important characteristic when studying a family's genogram. While birth order does not *predict* anything, it often explains at least some of the observed behaviors in these family systems. In many families, the eldest sibling is more used to determining direction or making decisions, while the middle or youngest sibling is more complacent, willing to go with the flow. While this is a generalization, the genogram may provide insights that help us understand why one family member consistently subordinates his or her own interests to follow another's lead — maybe with great resentment formed from childhood. This is particularly relevant when we look at enterprising families, because much may ride on sibling position. The oldest is often the first to get to the leadership table – if only because he or she is the oldest and so, perhaps, the first available to establish themselves in the family business, learn the skills, and be considered for succession. In some families, gender coupled with birth order can be the defining characteristics for a family (and family business) leadership position – i.e., the eldest son becomes the de facto successor leader.

The genogram can also expose a pattern of family member cutoffs (severed family relationships). Cutoffs run in families and will be discussed in greater detail in Chapter 10. The reason cutoffs typically appear in clusters is that a cutoff in one generation teaches the next generation that disposing of family relationships is an acceptable conflict management strategy. It is amazing how genograms of enterprising families often show a series of cutoffs in generation after generation. It is akin to tracing alcoholism or genetic afflictions in families – the afflictions re-occur generation after generation.

It is also useful to consider the "birth" of the business within the context of the birth order of children of enterprising families. Often the birth of a business demands so much attention and so many resources from its founder(s), typically one or both parents, that children born after the business formed have significantly different experiences of their parents and their parenting than do children born prior to the founding. So, it may be useful to include the business in the genogram among the constellation of siblings.

Understanding the Business Structure: The Organizational Chart

The org-chart of a business maps out the structure of the business. Using an org-chart as a tool to understand the business subsystem of the stakeholder map is very helpful, but it needs to be done within the context of the entire family business system to fully inform the conflict manager. Org-charts illustrate how organizations are designed: Who reports to whom, how functions are grouped, and how product or service areas are grouped are all shown graphically through a hierarchical or matrix-type structure. In non-family firms, the org-chart reliably shows the organizational hierarchy of the firm and identifies, fairly accurately, where power is held in the organization.

In a family-owned company, however, this is not always the case. Consider the org-chart in Figure 9-3 on the following page. Were this a non-family firm, it would be clear that the ultimate decision-making power rested with Tom, the CEO, and executives like Jeff, Bob, Steve, and Greg have power over their subordinate managers (Salah, Krissy, Alan, Arthur, and so on).

But, in a family-owned firm, that same org-chart might tell a different story. If the boxes for positions held by family members are shaded, it's less clear who holds real power. (See Figure 9-4, page 143.)

As the org-chart in Figure 9-4 now shows, in this case, Alan and Arthur are family members/owners. Is it realistic to think that Greg and Bob really have more power than their family owner subordinates? With Arthur in marketing being able to speak with his father, Tom the CEO, over dinner, might he have the power to undermine what his manager Greg dictated? Further complicating this, in a family business there often are others who are not even on the org-chart who wield power in the organization. Tom's wife and her brother (an owner), as well as Jeff's sister (whose husband Alan works at the firm), have a lot to say that can shift the balance of power.

Looking deeper at the org-chart, the conflict manager should determine whether there are clear job descriptions associated with the various roles. Similarly, it's important to note if real accountability exists. In family-owned and operated companies, there may be neither job descriptions nor accountability standards, and this vacuum, over time, can lead to conflict. In Chapter 7 we discussed structural development as an approach to managing conflict. In that context we suggested that clear policies regarding family employment and compensation be articulated. It is through the org-chart tool that these topics can be discussed and developed. With clearly articulated career paths and expectations for next-generation stakeholders, conflict around issues such as "fairness" and "entitlement behavior" can be managed.

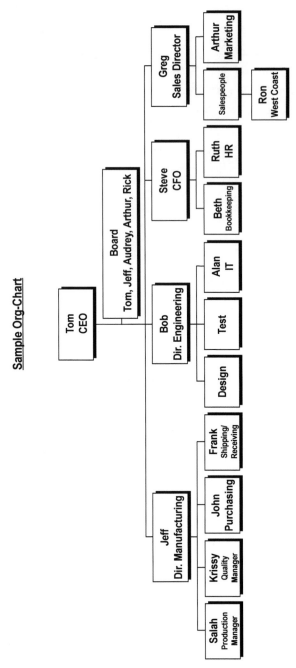

Sample Org-Chart

Figure 9-3

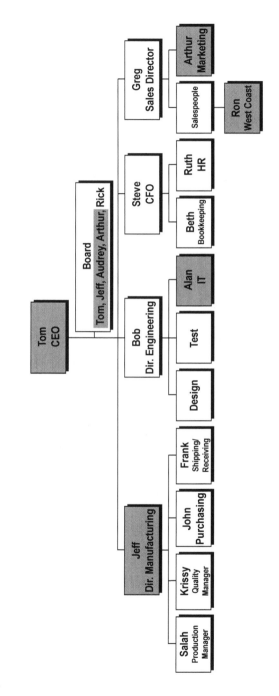

Sample Org-Chart with Family Relationships

Figure 9-4

Understanding Legal and Economic Connections: Document Checklist

A checklist showing which documents are available, up-to-date or non-existent can help the conflict manager keep track of individual stakeholders' rights and responsibilities under different circumstances. The devil is in the details and, that said, many family businesses have very few details spelled out. This can lead to even more conflict over time. To do a thorough job, the conflict manager should first determine if certain documents exist and, if they do, check to see whether they are up-to-date, well written and adequate to their purpose. A simple checklist like the one in Chapter 8 will guide the conflict manager to help the stakeholders clarify their understandings and put structures into place that will not only provide for future eventualities, but will serve to manage potential conflict in the future.

Understanding Family Enterprise Strategy: SWOT Analysis

One common method for evaluating external factors, as well as assessing the developmental condition of the business and its stakeholders, comes from traditional business consulting. The SWOT Analysis is the process of looking at a company's strategic strengths, weaknesses, opportunities, and threats. Strategic strengths and weaknesses are intrinsic to the business in question and, to a large extent, within the control of that organization's leadership. Opportunities and threats, however, may come from sources beyond the direct control of any stakeholder. The only thing that stakeholders can do is to prepare for these contingencies and choose responses when they become relevant.

For traditional business enterprises, opportunities and threats come from the marketplace, the economy, regulators, technological advances, and natural disasters. In a family business, however, it is necessary to also consider opportunities and threats coming from the family, which may impact the business system. These may include illness and accidents affecting key individuals, marriages, divorces, births or graduations, for example.

SWOT Analysis also requires looking inward to the strengths and weaknesses of the company and its people. It provides the conflict manager with an organized way to consider whether the company has the processes, strategies, and people in place to be competitive. This effort speaks directly to the structural and personal development approach to managing conflict we discussed in Chapter 7. When the company lacks clarity regarding how things get done or has people who are insufficiently trained or skilled in roles of responsibility, conflict can breed. Developing those systems, and the stakeholders involved in those systems, is among the most effective ways to manage conflict in a family business.

Although SWOT Analysis was primarily designed for evaluating businesses, this same approach can be used to evaluate the family system. In this case, opportunities and threats to the family may come from the business or from how wealth is made available. A SWOT Analysis is a powerful tool to evaluate any of the family enterprise systems depicted on the Stakeholder Map (see Figure 9-5) and it should be considered for each of these systems.

Stakeholder Map™
for Family Business

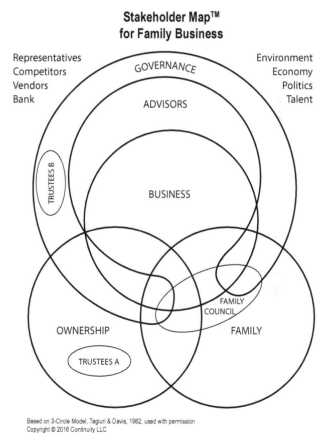

Based on 3-Circle Model, Tagiuri & Davis, 1982, used with permission
Copyright © 2016 Continuity LLC

Figure 9-5

Understanding Stakeholder Roles: The Stakeholder Map

We first mentioned the Stakeholder Map in Chapter 3 when we explained the systemic nature of the family business system. The Stakeholder Map is a snapshot in time. It shows who sits where in the family enterprise system currently. It can also be used for future planning by using arrows to depict movement among the various subsystems. The map illustrates the individual subsystems in which family business stakeholders reside. These subsystems are: family, business, ownership, governance (both business and family), trustee and advisory. These subsystems sit in a larger external universe, namely the world around them, through which they are affected by a myriad of other factors.

Not only does the Stakeholder Map (see Figure 9-5) show the interdependence among stakeholders residing in different parts of the system, it also sheds light regarding an individual's likely concerns and motivations that may be related to the overlapping roles they play. An individual who is a family member and an owner of the business might care more about shareholder distributions from the business than a family member who is an employee and not an owner of the business. That family member may be more concerned about retaining cash in the business for future growth and ample salaries and perks. It is easy to see how conflict can be generated by the concerns and motivations associated with each stakeholder role in the family enterprise.

This map shows the eight subsystems described in this chapter, including the universe in which the business operates. With over two dozen unique combinations of roles, it is striking to see how complicated family roles and responsibilities are. This means that there are thousands of potential situations for unique interdependent relationships in a large family business. Since the potential for conflict increases as interdependence increases, there is a wealth of opportunity for conflict to breed in a family enterprise. Because each unique role carries with it a unique set of typical motivations and concerns that may be at odds with those in other roles, it is no surprise that conflict in family enterprise is so ubiquitous.

While understanding the map is complicated, using it is not. The conflict manager simply writes each stakeholder's name or initials into the space where he or she resides. The more individuals who simultaneously participate in several systems, the more interdependence there is, and thus the more potential for conflict.

The value of the Stakeholder Map is that it shows on one piece of paper where all stakeholders (or stakeholder groups) sit in the system. By adding arrows to show potential movement of stakeholders within the map, a succession or exit plan can be depicted. Understanding how each stakeholder role corresponds to likely motivations and concerns will help the conflict manager anticipate potential structural, or systemic, conflict.

The Family System

Families come in all shapes and sizes and they bring with them unique dynamics. Defining the family system is pretty straightforward. It is composed of all the family members, whether or not they are involved in the business. This includes in-laws, stepchildren, and adopted children. Family wealth planning may actually include children who are not yet born. In addition, family governance policies (such as the need for prenuptial agreements) may refer to future spouses. (As we noted earlier, the genogram is a particularly useful tool for understanding the family subsystem.)

The Business System

The business subsystem also is straightforward – everyone who works in the business is part of this system. For simplicity's sake, we generally only include key non-family managers on the Stakeholder Map, but include all family members working full-time in the business, regardless of their role. The business subsystem will range from simple to complex depending on the nature and size of the enterprise. Some businesses may be complex structures with multiple divisions, or conglomerates consisting of many diverse companies. Family offices are also included in the business system as are significant assets, like vacation properties, that are shared among family. The Stakeholder Map is intended to be used with individual business entities. More complex company structures may require the use of multiple Stakeholder Maps. Within each business unit, the org-chart and ownership schedules can be good tools to understand how each business is structured.

The Ownership System

This subsystem includes everyone who owns any portion of the shared enterprise. Ownership systems of family enterprises range from extremely simple sole proprietorships to highly complex systems with multiple owners, different classes of stock, ownership by various trusts, and employee stock option plans (ESOPs). For the purpose of managing conflict, the conflict manager should consider *all* owners — not just the current, outright, majority owners, but also the minority and potential future owners of all classes of stock. Ownership may not be represented by shares, but may be represented by agreements and promises made. Ownership can be in a business organization or among shared assets like commercial real estate or a family vacation property.

Of all the conflicts in a family business system, arguments over ownership can be the most extreme. Unanswerable questions of "what is fair" abound when families try to decide how to apportion ownership to a rising generation of siblings and cousins. Vague promises of ownership, issues of entitlement, lack of a true understanding of the benefits and risks of ownership (e.g., tax exposure), minority rights, and a host of other issues can become fodder for many a lawsuit and therefore must be carefully evaluated.

Similarly, the ramifications of gifting ownership in an operating company to all siblings or cousins when only some of them work in the business should be carefully considered. The conflict manager needs to understand the types of stock, trusts, and agreements that are in place. Addressing these specific challenges is beyond the scope of this book, but it is important to mention these issues, as they can become sources of conflict for enterprising families. The key to understanding past, current and future ownership is in the documentation of buy-sell agreements and estate plans, but also in examining individuals' expectations and histories.

How Does Ownership Complexity Evolve?

There are several ways to finance the start of a business. An entrepreneur can start small, borrow a bit of money and grow a business over time while retaining complete ownership and control. Businesses can be started with multiple owners: as partnerships or by selling capital in exchange for an ownership stake to investors. Sometimes, partnerships can be forged with family members, making the business an instant family business. Other times, non-family members end up with ownership stakes and may retain those stakes over generations. It is important for the conflict manager to understand the history of the company's ownership, as it provides great insight into the culture surrounding the ownership of the business.

It is not uncommon for the conflict manager to find that companies have gotten off to a rocky start regarding ownership. Siblings may have battled for control of the business and a buyout of one or more branches may have occurred in the past – leaving damaged family relationships in its wake. Some non-family and family owners may have chosen to sell out, been forced out, or perhaps been bought out after a protracted legal battle. Ownership of some type may have been provided or promised to non-family stakeholders as an employment incentive or in exchange for intellectual property. Ownership complexity may also develop due to the merger of different companies. Because the history of ownership is carried within the mind-set of the current owners, their willingness to consider outside investment, or to transition ownership to the rising generation, may be influenced by past experience – for good or for ill.

Some owners may have inherited the stock through no effort or commitment of their own and may see the value of their ownership as they would view any other financial investment. They may not identify strongly with ownership of the family business or feel committed to its legacy. Alternatively, some owners may have grown up in the shadow of the business, devoted their careers to it, and may thus feel both entitled to ownership and committed to employment in the company. Some stakeholders may view ownership as an important personal connection to family and history that is, to some extent, critical to their identity.

In addition to history, personality can play a major role in ownership systems. An owner may place excessive value on having complete control and be reluctant to part with any stock. Conversely, an owner may be interested in sharing ownership with others in exchange for meaningful contribution or to perpetuate family ownership and legacy.

How stakeholders feel about their current or potential future ownership of the family business can be as important as how much of the company they actually own or will own. In fact, stakeholders may not be owners at all, but may act like owners or feel entitled to ownership based on their contributions to the business or promises made to them in the past. The conflict manager must consider even these stakeholders in evaluating the ownership system as their anticipated ownership plays a part in the conflict system.

Ownership as Power

Depending on how the business is structured, ownership can come with or without voting rights. Even with voting rights, however, minority shareholders may feel powerless, unable to influence the company's direction, policies, leadership or operations. As previously mentioned, minority rights vary by state, but they generally offer minority shareholders some power by holding the majority shareholders to reasonable standards of fiduciary duty to the minority. This means that a disgruntled minority shareholder might be able to use the court system if they feel they have been wronged. Whether or not a good case exists, even the threat of a protracted, public court process might be an effective source of power. However, being a family business means that relationships matter, and we believe that families should do whatever they can to prevent legal battles. Keep in mind that litigation is likely to be seen as the use of Disrespected Power and the result may only be to trigger ever more conflict.

What is Fair?

How much stock should next-generation stakeholders get? Who deserves more? How much control of the business should each next-generation stakeholder get? How much financial benefit? Does stock ownership carry risk and/or responsibility? To whom should the benefits of future corporate growth accrue? There is no one answer to any of these questions. Families agonize over these questions and often delay making decisions about transferring ownership until it's too late.

But what is *fair*? The search for fairness is often a dead end. Just as "fair" doesn't necessarily mean "equal," "equal" may not actually be fair – especially to the sibling who believes he or she has contributed more, and who sees themselves as crucial to the growth of the business. "Equal" may not be fair to the family branch that has a special-needs child or who needs extraordinary financial support. "Equal" may also not be perceived as fair to the non-employed family shareholder who thinks that those working in the business are getting disproportionate benefit through salaries, perks and career opportunity. Or, "equal" may not be considered fair to those working in the business who believe the non-employed shareholders are contributing nothing but are benefitting from their own hard work in the business. Perhaps equal financial benefit may be considered fair for one family, but is equal control over the family business fair to the stakeholders who have committed their careers to the business and may have their livelihood put at risk by shareholders who may want to liquidate the company or stifle investment for growth in favor of greater distributions?

In the search to find fairness, the concept of "rough equalization" has developed. This involves considering all the family assets, not just the business, and providing a larger share of ownership and control of the business to those who contribute to its growth and who have made a significant career and personal commitment to it. Other assets that may not have the growth potential of the business but may be less risky are given in larger share to those who are not as active in or dependent on the business. While there may not be significant other assets (and this strategy is not recommended for all families), it is something to be considered.

The concern, however, is that if the business becomes very successful (likely due to the efforts of those in charge) and thus exceedingly valuable, the siblings who did not inherit the shares may feel they were unfairly treated because they were unable to profit from the growth of that asset. Similarly, if the business fails, the siblings who *did* inherit the business may feel they were treated unfairly because they were given a flawed asset and now have no share in the family's beachfront vacation home.

The point is that "fair" is a loaded word, a false promise, and an unachievable goal. Rough equalization is all that can be hoped for. A family with a strong Family Factor and the ability to manage conflict well will be able to manage wealth disparity as it develops so that the family remains strong and connected.

The Corporate Governance System

Both family and non-family, owner and non-owner directors populate the corporate governance area of the Stakeholder Map. Sometimes key executives or trustees might also be directors. The important thing to understand about directors is that they have a fiduciary duty to represent the interests of *all* the company owners — and they have the power of their vote on the board to do so. Family businesses are generally, but not always, "controlled board" companies where independent directors cannot outvote what the owners want concerning most important issues.

Families sometimes use advisory boards as a substitute for independent fiduciary boards. Advisory boards are simpler and less expensive than fiduciary boards and this is why they are attractive to family business stakeholders. Advisory board members, however, do not have a fiduciary duty to shareholders. They are simply advisors with no power and no responsibility. Because of this, advisory boards can be useful, but they do not offer families the real help in managing conflict that fiduciary boards offer. Because they hold no power or official status, advisory board members appear in the "advisory" subsystem, not the "governance" subsystem of the stakeholder map.

Directors of any business, family-owned or not, have the same basic set of responsibilities. By representing *all* shareholders, board members provide oversight and approve corporate strategy, capital expenditures and distribution policy. They also review key executive performance and compensation, advise on merger and acquisition opportunities, and ensure that proper management and board succession planning is in place.

For the board of a family business, however, these responsibilities include not only oversight regarding the strategic threats and opportunities in the marketplace, but also those arising from family issues. Births, deaths, marriages, divorces, graduations and a host of other family events and issues may have enormous impact on the strategic direction and security of the company.

Board members must also be prepared to deal with many of the inherent conflicts that arise from the overlapping systems as shown on the Stakeholder Map. Family branches fighting over control, under-skilled family members who are in line for succession, family members expecting inappropriate compensation, and a host of other issues are likely to be board topics in a family business. Good family governance, such as family councils, can be used to sort out some family employment or ownerships issues so that they do not overwhelm the corporate governance board. However, in a family business, outside directors should have relevant family business experience and anticipate that some family issues will come to the board.

Who's on the Board?

Most family business boards begin as statutory boards that rarely meet and serve a limited purpose. At some point, the board might expand to include a few family members and perhaps a trusted advisor. Eventually, however, a more proactive effort is made to craft a board that meets the needs of the preponderance of family enterprise stakeholders.

In early generation or founder-run businesses, the last thing most CEO/owners want is to be accountable to a board – especially when the CEO/owner is also the majority stockholder. While it may seem to be against his or her own interests to be subordinate to a board, the leader who can understand and accept the guidelines and responsibilities of good governance will reap great rewards. Even without seating a formal board, simply holding oneself accountable to professional governance standards may be the first step towards effective governance.

At some point, however, populating the board with appropriate outside (i.e., non-family) directors can prove transformative for the company and its family owners. One particularly strong advantage of independent boards is for family businesses that are transitioning from the founder generation to a generation with both family owners and family managers in the company. An independent board, with professional corporate governance structure, policy and practice, is more likely to be able to hold family managers accountable to non-employed owners. They are more likely to provide a level of transparency and confidence for family owners who do not work at the business.

The Family Governance System

Family governance, also known as a family council, is a subsystem within the family system. That means that all family council members will also be family members. In large multigenerational family enterprises, the family governance system can have great influence on the family business system.

Families are organized systems, quite similar in many aspects to business systems. So it is logical that families might also benefit from a system of governance. In fact, many families that do not have a business or significant shared wealth that binds them together, often have strong family governance systems. They may hold yearly retreats where they discuss issues of concern to the extended family. They may take annual vacations together as extended family, or they may get together for holidays, family transitions, and celebrations. Families may stay connected through newsletters or communicate frequently through online groups. Those who initiate, organize, and plan for these events are performing family governance functions. They may be part of a well-organized, formal family council with by-laws, voting procedures and acknowledged leaders. Or, their events may develop organically with informal leadership.

Family councils can be extremely effective in helping enterprising families develop leaders, grow their collective wealth, and provide support for family members with problems and challenges in their lives. They can also communicate with the family business board to provide the information the board needs in order to understand the family's interests and to plan for possible strategic threats and/or opportunities arising from within the family.

Certain documents, including family vision, mission, statement of values, or even a family constitution are useful in keeping a family connected and aligned in their decision-making. A family council is where these documents are developed. A family, united through good family governance, can leverage relationships and family capital to create a competitive advantage as an enterprising family.

The Advisory System

In a perfect world, the inhabitants of the advisory subsystem would each be truly independent from (have no overlap with) the other subsystems. Advisors would serve no role beyond advising the family or the business in some specific, limited capacity. This means that they would not also be family members, owners, managers, trustees or directors. When advisors have dual roles as stakeholder and advisor, they can easily become conflicted or biased.

The trouble is that this rule is often not followed. Corporate attorneys are routinely given a role as a director or trustee. Family members with the right credentials often serve as investment advisors, financial advisors, or CPAs. This doesn't always pose a problem, but when conflict arises, advisors with dual or multiple roles can cause conflict to escalate.

Conversely, having a full complement of competent, unbiased, non-conflicted advisors can be extremely effective in managing conflict and making sure it doesn't escalate. When overlap of an advisory role and a stakeholder role is unavoidable, care must be taken to ensure that the overlap is managed. Clear rules regarding when a potentially conflicted or biased advisor or stakeholder should recuse themselves from a vote or service should be agreed upon. Documentation should include a contingency plan when advisory roles and stakeholder roles overlap and a conflict of interest exists.

Good family business advisors understand that family businesses are complex and that they cannot and should not attempt to provide for all its advisory needs. Rather, each advisor should possess collaborative skills, enabling them to work well on an advisory team. A good advisor will know when a family needs help outside his or her own area of expertise, and will initiate the call for collaborative professional advisors when needed.

Advisors who try to inappropriately limit the introduction of other professionals to their clients in order to protect what they consider to be their own turf can unwittingly send their clients down a destructive path. Sometimes these advisors expand their services beyond their area of expertise, which can hinder the productive evolution of the family business system. Keeping advisors conflict-free – i.e., not holding overlapping roles — will help keep them unbiased in their advice and encourage them to engage with other professionals for needed skill sets.

The Trustee System

The role of a trustee in a family business system is complex. Decisions regarding who should be a trustee should be made with a full understanding of potential conflicts of interest and the complex challenges and risks inherent in the role. Trusteeships generally exist as subsystems of the ownership system. When the trust controls only liquid wealth or fungible property, the role can be pretty straightforward, as it can be outlined without ambiguity in the trust documents.

When a trust owns stock in the family business, however, the trustee's role becomes much more complex. The intention may be for the trustee to keep the family business stock as a legacy holding, but the trust document may also require the trustee to make decisions to manage risk and maximize the value of the trust. In order to maintain a diversified portfolio, a concentrated holding in family business stock may not be able to be justified by the trustee. Trust documentation, therefore, should provide appropriate carve-outs enabling the trustee to hold concentrated positions in family company stock.

In addition, a trustee may have voting rights assigned to the company shares in trust, or the trustee may have a corporate board seat as directed by the trust. A trustee-director has a particularly thorny conflict of interest. On the one hand, he or she has the duty to promote the interests of the beneficiaries of the trust above anything else. But, as a director, the trustee has a duty to make decisions in the best interests of all shareholders. Managing these roles is not easy, and is beyond the scope of this book. But, trust documentation must take these potential conflicts of interest into account.

Although family members can serve as trustees, when they act as trustees, they are required to take their family "hat" off and follow the rules outlined in the trust agreement. For this reason, we depict the trustee role as existing only in the ownership and governance subsystems.

External Universe

A complete depiction of the subsystems involved in family business also includes the environment in which the family business system sits. This may include such constituencies as customers, competitors, bankers, and regulators, among others. Including these in the Stakeholder Map is essential for understanding the family business system.

Summary

A structure where some family members are owners of the business and other family members are managers in the business is fertile ground for misunderstanding and conflict. Shareholders may be primarily concerned with dividend distributions. Managers may be more concerned with higher salaries, bonuses, perks and reinvestment in the business. While such conflicting interests exist in all businesses, these differences take on larger significance when stakeholders are related, playing multiple roles that interface on different fronts and may carry over expectations, beliefs and even emotions from previous wearers of those hats.

- Tools exist to help the conflict manager understand and manage the complexity embedded in the family enterprise system.
- The genogram helps the conflict manager organize the complexity of the family subsystem. It provides graphical insight into many components of conflict that may exist in the family system.
- The org-chart helps the conflict manager understand how the business is organized and where power is held in the business subsystem.
- The document checklist helps the conflict manager understand where power is held, how stakeholders are interdependent, and provides insight into the enterprise system's existing level of structural development.
- The SWOT Analysis, applied to all subsystems of the family enterprise, helps the conflict manager assess the strategic health of the entire family enterprise system.
- The Stakeholder Map gives a comprehensive view of all subsystems and illustrates graphically the level of stakeholder interdependence in the family business system. It is useful as a planning tool to describe where stakeholders might move to within the family enterprise system.

Chapter 10

The Psychology of Enterprising Families

If you cannot get rid of the family skeleton, you may as well make it dance.
— George Bernard Shaw

Enterprising families are emotional systems, and our description of the family enterprise would not be complete without addressing the unique psychology that connects stakeholders to each other and drives their motivations and concerns from an emotional and psychological perspective. Any discussion of conflict and its management must be informed by the psychological system that connects stakeholder motivations and concerns to their behavior.

In *Anna Karenina*, Leo Tolstoy wrote "All happy families are alike; each unhappy family is unhappy in its own way." We echo that by saying that all families are alike; each enterprising family is exceptional in its own way. Being an enterprising family adds a significant level of complexity to the structure of the family. As we have described in the previous chapters, this complexity brings with it opportunities as well as challenges. While successful enterprising family members are able to take advantage of the opportunities, others may find it hard to overcome the challenges.

As a group, enterprising family members have many advantages over other families. In some cases, a family name may be well-known in their community through a business or charitable foundation, or in political and social circles. Rising generation members accordingly have access to people and opportunities that may be unavailable to others and this access can lead to unparalleled social, academic or professional opportunities. When the family business or wealth is discussed at home, these children are exposed at a young age to business thinking, decision-making and financial literacy in ways others would not be. The opportunity to travel internationally at a young age provides a worldliness that can build character and confidence. Access to summer jobs, often with more responsibility than others would have, also gives rising generation members opportunities that can help them get jobs at other companies should they want them, or a secure career path to leadership in their family enterprise. Finally, access to the best educational opportunities and experiences gives rising generations of enterprising families a competitive edge in our world.

As a result, members of enterprising families have, on the face of it, extraordinary opportunities to make them better educated, connected, and more worldly than their compatriots from non-enterprising families. But, all those open doors come with a price.

In this chapter, we discuss some of the psychological and emotional challenges that sometimes face stakeholders in enterprising families. The challenges we identify derive from our observations from working with many families, rather than from statistical analysis. Our purpose in presenting these observations, therefore, is to help stakeholders and their advisors increase their awareness of these challenges so, to paraphrase Ernest Hemingway, stakeholders can *make strong what their world may weaken.*

Many stakeholders have naturally accommodated, avoided or overcome these challenges, and nothing in this chapter is intended to imply that any individual stakeholder is impacted by these challenges. As family business consultants, we get called when something is awry in the family business system. This logically gives rise to a bias in our observations – we meet families where things are not perfect. This chapter provides readers with the benefits of our observations from this admittedly biased sample.

Bowen Family Systems Theory

A psychological framework that is especially informative for enterprising families was introduced by Dr. Murray Bowen in the 1950s. Having studied Freudian psychoanalysis, Bowen came to believe that instead of individual behavior being dictated by unresolved issues within their individual psyches, actions and motivations were better understood as rooted in the family system. Bowen Family Systems Theory suggests that individuals cannot be understood in isolation from their family of origin.

In the context of his theory, Bowen suggests that we can learn much about people when we understand the circumstances of their upbringing. Did they have brothers and sisters? Where did they fall in the birth order? What were the relative age differences? Was it a big, multigenerational family with lots of cousins, aunts, uncles and seniors? What were the defining events in the lives of the stakeholders that marked their transitions into adulthood? How do in-laws perceive the family and how are they treated by the family? How are conflict and stress managed in the family? The answers to these questions are relevant to several of the components of *The Conflict Equation*.

Bowen Family Systems Theory identifies eight concepts that should be considered when trying to understand the individuals that make up the family:

1. Differentiation of Self
2. Triangles
3. Nuclear Family Emotional Process
4. Family Projection Process
5. Cutoff
6. Multigenerational Transmission Process
7. Sibling Position
8. Societal Emotional Process

While a thorough description of each of these eight concepts is beyond the scope of this book, we offer a brief description along with the particular impact that each concept exerts on the enterprising family. Keep in mind that the enterprising family is one that is connected by significant economic opportunity and often includes families who work closely together in multigenerational businesses. These economic and professional ties overlay family relationships, multiplying the impact of each of the concepts within the Bowen framework.

Bowen Family Systems Theory refers to the family that one grows up with as one's family of origin. The family that one starts as an adult is referred to as one's nuclear family. Your nuclear family, for example, will be your child's family of origin.

Differentiation of Self

In a typical family, children grow up in their family of origin, achieve some level of education, find their professional or vocational calling, find a job that will support their personal goals, move away from the home they grew up in, and start their own lives, developing their own nuclear families. In this way, children leave the nest, become their own individual selves and begin their own independent families. Although they usually retain relationships with their parents and siblings, the child has gone through a process of individuation – of finding out who they are independently from their family of origin. In Bowenian terms, this is referred to as *self-differentiation*. In adulthood, they are able to redefine their relationships with their parents and siblings as adults, differentiated from who they were as children. This is an essential challenge of becoming an adult.

In the enterprising family, be it a family of wealth or one with a family business at the core of the family's economy, children may face particular challenges as they negotiate their path to adulthood that make it harder for them to follow the above scenario. The pull of family wealth, or of the opportunity in the family business, can be so strong that it can keep children integrated in their family of origin at the precise time they need to separate and differentiate. In some enterprising families, the fear of losing opportunity may keep the child from straying too far, or from taking the necessary risks to find out who they are meant to be. In others, the sheer magnitude of an opportunity that dwarfs what the child perceives he or she could accomplish on their own keeps him/her enmeshed in their family of origin.

In these families, successful differentiation can be exceedingly difficult. The child may choose a field of study not because they are truly interested in that subject, but because it is compatible with the opportunity afforded by the family. In some families the child works in the family business during holiday breaks and summers. In others they don't work at all and live off family wealth. In short, children in enterprising families have the possibility of avoiding the very experiences that would challenge them and help them differentiate from their family of origin.

Instead of differentiating, many conform – even reluctantly. Others, however, may rebel against these opportunities and expectations and seek out paths expressly for the purpose of not being in the family business – but also not for the purpose of finding their true calling. Still others may never experience the need to figure out their place in the world and this can rob them of the needed opportunity for psychological growth.

For some of these children, this strategy or path works out well and they lead happy lives. Some manage to differentiate well and overcome these challenges. Others figure out how to adapt and be productive despite a lower level of self-differentiation. For others, however, it can become problematic to approach adult-hood without having made the important transition of letting go of their family of origin to strike out on their own path in life. Lacking this opportunity to re-engage with their family of origin as adults, their childhood and adolescent relationships with sib-lings, parents and cousins, can extend into their adult years.

Historically, when family was part of a tribe or a clan, ex-traordinary and elaborate rites of passage were developed to en-able children to pass into adulthood while not physically leaving the tribe. As a society, we mostly have lost these rites of passage. Today's norm is for children to head off to college and to travel great distances to develop their careers. For these children, for-mal rites of passage may be less important; time and distance do the trick. Maybe college and relocation are today's rites of passage. But children of enterprising families typically stay con-nected to a much more significant degree, which can keep the child from fully differentiating.

Children who are less differentiated as adults may bring a host of problems into their own nuclear families and into the family busi-ness system. They often crave acknowledgement because they are still in the parent-child environment where that is a normal need. Under-differentiated adults tend not to be able to deal with conflict well because they haven't fully integrated who they truly are with the outside world. They also tend to have entangled or "enmeshed" relationships between their family of origin and their nuclear fami-ly, causing conflict and stress to spread like wildfire.

We often hear from people who married into enterpris-ing families that they were unprepared for the challenges they faced entering their spouse's family. Or, we'll hear, "Everyone is in everyone else's personal business." Relationships within the in-law's (non-enterprising) family are generally comparatively calm and predictable. Siblings tend to treat each other as adults, and have reasonable boundaries and pleasant relationships, more so than in the enterprising family.

Certainly, not all enterprising families are as problematic as we have described. We only suggest that these behaviors are more likely in enterprising families than in non-enterprising families. Being able to identify levels of differentiation and family enmeshment is a valuable skill for a conflict manager in a family business setting, as they can point to opportunities for stakeholder, and family, development.

Triangles

When two people, or a dyad, are in conflict, stress and pressure build up until there is a breaking point. At that point, either the relationship ends, or a third person is brought in to relieve some of the pressure. That third person stabilizes the dyad, although not necessarily in a healthy way, and enables that relationship – and its dysfunction — to continue. A two-legged stool will easily fall over when something pushes it off balance. A third leg adds stability in the same manner that a third person adds stability to a problematic relationship.

In the more enmeshed enterprising family, where individuals are connected by blood, business and wealth, triangulation is the norm. Breaking the dyad, or ending relationships with family, is so unthinkable and impractical that a third person (or family branch) is dragged in to keep the conflict going, and the relationships stable.

In healthy families, these triangles form and change fluidly. When, however, these triangles get stuck, and family branches turn into factions or one person forever becomes the go-between, opportunities for family development abound.

Nuclear Family Emotional Process

Anxiety and stress manifest in many ways in the nuclear family. Much of this anxiety comes from the natural process of the differentiation of children. Families have identifiable emotional processes that they go through in dealing with this anxiety. One family member may become disconnected as a result of the stress, anxiety, and conflict. Another family member may overcompensate for the other and become the spokesperson for that disconnected family member.

Family Projection Process

One manifestation of the Nuclear Family Emotional Process discussed above occurs when parents project their emotional problems onto their children. In this scenario, anxiety and conflict in the parents' relationship becomes focused on the child and the child is seen as the problem. Often, when parents focus on their own problems with each other in the relationship, the child's behavior somehow ceases to be the problem.

Again, when these relationships involve a functioning business or economic entity, the results can be far-reaching for the entire family business system.

Emotional Cutoff

When conflict becomes severe, as it so frequently can in family enterprise, it sometimes happens that certain family members cease all interaction with the family, or with sections of the family. This is called a "cutoff." The blood, emotional, financial and legal bonds may still exist, but contact and communication have ceased.

An individual who desires to cut him or herself off from the family can initiate the cessation of contact, or the family can decide to isolate itself from the individual. Cutoffs can involve not just individuals, but entire branches or other groupings.

Enterprising families are often connected by legal agreements and shared financial assets, so attempts at cutoff can be very difficult to maintain in totality. In addition, cutoffs typically do not impact the entire family. Conduits of contact are often maintained with some family members or third-party intermediaries.

The problem with cutoffs is that they run in families. They teach the lesson to subsequent generations that cutting off communication with family members is an acceptable approach to managing conflict in the family. This is why when we see cutoffs in a family, we tend to see their recurrence through the generations.

Multigenerational Transmission Process

"The apple doesn't fall far from the tree." This all-too-true proverb resonates with the Bowen Family Systems perspective. Highly functional parents breed children who likely differentiate well and employ the valuable lessons learned from their parents to raise high-functioning children of their own. Parents who have low levels of self-differentiation typically maintain highly enmeshed families where stress and anxiety build up, causing cutoffs and continued challenges to differentiation in their offspring.

Of course, every individual has the power to escape this fate, and coming from a well-developed family does not ensure any individual's successful differentiation. It's just that the odds are better for subsequent generations when the dysfunctional cycles are broken. Enterprising families may be more prone to these challenges, but they also have the resources available to address these challenges once they are aware of them.

Sibling Position

Bowen theory has much to say about birth order, much of it based on the research of Walter Toman. From Bowen's perspective, so much of our personalities and skill sets develop from the birth order and sibling universe in which we were raised. Birth order, sibling count, and gender are not predictive, but they are influential. Understanding these characteristics of a stakeholder's upbringing frequently explains many observed behaviors and can provide the conflict manager with extremely useful insight into each stakeholder.

Birth order is far from an exact science and it does not predict any individual's behavior. However, the conflict manager can better understand each individual from the perspective of their sibling universe. And, each individual can achieve valuable insights into his/her own behavior, and the behaviors of all family members, through the lens of sibling rank, gender, age disparity, and sibling count.

In a family business, sibling relationships are often the front lines of conflict. When stakeholders understand the influence that the characteristics of their sibling universe have had on each stakeholder, they can often understand problematic behavior as structural, to some extent, rather than personal.

Societal Emotional Process

The societal emotional process describes a somewhat reciprocal relationship whereby not only is a family impacted by changes in the greater society, but societal institutions such as governments, workplaces, and schools are impacted by aggregate changes in families.

We believe this element of Bowen's framework affirms our thinking as we believe that enterprising families are impacted by their enterprise and vice versa. To family enterprise stakeholders reading this book, this insight will likely seem obvious. When a business or a family's wealth becomes such an influential factor in a family's life, as it can be in many enterprising families, the stresses and demands that arise in those areas can pervade the family and impact the development of the family. Similarly, stresses and demands in the family can impact how its enterprise operates and evolves.

Psychologist Urie Bronfenbrenner, in his 1979 "Theory of Human Ecology," supported this understanding when he wrote about the various systems that influence childhood development in addition to the family system. Although he spoke mainly about the influence of schooling, for anyone raised with a family business, it is easy to see how family enterprise can compete with schooling as an influential factor in childhood development.

Beyond Bowen Family Theory

Bowen's framework helps connect the emotional and behavioral dots among stakeholders when family members work and share together as adults, thereby offering tremendously useful insight to a conflict manager. In addition to the elements described in Bowen's theory, there are many other factors that affect the psychology of enterprising families.

In-Laws

Much has been written about in-laws in examining family business – much of it negative. "Married-ins" have been derided as instigators of conflict and denigrated as "out-laws." The truth is that in-laws can play powerful roles in enterprising families. They can be destructive forces and catalysts for cutoffs and family wars, or they can be unifying forces, providing a healthy sense of perspective to their new extended families.

Some families seek to minimize the impact of in-laws on the family business system and institute elaborate rules of engagement for sequestering the influence of spouses of family stakeholders. Often such rules are futile, as in-laws impact the system regardless.

An in-law comes to a family as a point of fusion between two families. He or she enters the family business system with limited experience regarding the history and dynamics that exist in the system. They often end up asking, "what have I gotten myself into" when they finally experience these dynamics firsthand.

It's possible to look at marriages, and their impact on the family business system, through the lens of Bowen Family Systems Theory. Marriages, in which one of the partners is still enmeshed with their family of origin, can face enormous challenges. If one partner has a lower level of self-differentiation, as may be more common in enterprising families, that partner might feel compelled to draw their spouse into his or her own family-of-origin drama. They may expect their spouse, the in-law, to be upset when they are upset, and to engage in other enmeshed family behaviors. They may feel betrayed when the in-law takes a more rational, less emotional look at a problem concerning their family of origin, or when the in-law suggests that they reduce the time spent with his/her spouse's family of origin.

All individuals develop unique communication and coping behaviors that sustain relationships with their families of origin. Because relationships among family members of enterprising families may be potentially more enmeshed, these communication and coping behaviors may be unusually intense, emotional, and complicated. In addition, higher levels of fused relationships (triangles and enmeshment) raise the overall level of anxiety, reactivity and emotionality in the systems. An in-law may simply not be prepared for this. The in-law may not understand how the spouse's family-of-origin system operates. What may be a "normal" equilibrium in the enterprising family may be perceived by the new in-law as difficult, or entirely unacceptable.

The fact is, however, that in-laws often do bring valuable insight and perspective to the family business system. Since they may not come from an enterprising family, they may naturally be more self-differentiated than their spouse, who has had the challenge of trying to self-differentiate within the family business system. The in-law may see things more objectively and less emotionally (i.e., more rationally). What the in-law identifies as unacceptable behavior may indeed be damaging to his or her spouse, unfair, and even toxic to the healthy functioning of their current nuclear family. The in-law may be the "voice of reason" in a sea of emotional chaos, the one providing an objective perspective for the family. So why is the in-law typically ineffective in helping the family manage conflict? Why do their well-meaning efforts often trigger more conflict?

In-laws are simply in the wrong position to effect much positive change because they have an obvious stake in the outcome of the family drama. The value of an independent neutral party cannot be overstated when it comes to managing any conflict – especially family business conflict with its highly reactive and emotional subtext. When the in-law attempts to get involved in the family business drama, they are often met with accusations of meddling, and their arguments or observations are dismissed as biased, purely self-interested, or worse.

In addition, when in-laws get involved in family business drama, they often put their spouse in the position of having to choose: nuclear family over his or her family of origin – a terrible dilemma, especially for the potentially under-differentiated individual. This decision becomes exponentially more complicated when it also involves ownership, career, and inheritance related to the family business or shared wealth. This only serves to raise the overall level of anxiety in the system, causing further dysfunction and conflict.

The conflict manager should look toward in-laws as potential treasure troves of relatively objective knowledge about family relationships and behavior. While many fingers may be pointed at the in-law for instigating disputes and cutoffs, in-laws should not be demonized. The role of the in-law is difficult and fraught with the potential to make matters worse, rather than better, despite good intentions.

The conflict manager can help married-ins better understand their role in the family business system – its challenges, limitations, and resources. Diffusing conflict emanating from the in-law relationship is crucial in the management of family business conflict. For this reason, having in-laws participate in the conflict management process is essential.

Wealth Disparity

Another issue that is critical to understanding an enterprising family is wealth disparity. When siblings grow up in similar economic circumstances, but then end up living with very different levels of wealth as adults, much changes. Similarly, when one sibling has significantly more children than the others, the relative wealth finding its way to the cousins' generation, from trust distributions or the inheritance of the business or wealth, may be dramatically different. Wealth disparity among family stakeholders, especially within the same generation, can be a source of significant conflict.

Wealth often drives stakeholder motivations and concerns and, thus, goals. Wealth can shape stakeholder values. Different levels of wealth are capable, therefore, of driving different goals and values among stakeholders. When goals and values are different among stakeholders, it is possible that some of the goals may be in opposition and some of the values may be incompatible.

To illustrate what happens in families, consider when the shares of a successful family enterprise are divided equally among four siblings (each then owns 25%) and then they equally divide their shares among their children. If three siblings have two children each (those cousins own 12.5%) and one sibling has seven children (they each own 3.5%), wealth disparity at the cousin level will exist. Accordingly, imagine if on an annual basis the company distributes $2 million. Cousins owning 12.5% would receive a $250,000 distribution, while those with 3.5% would receive just $70,000. This is not to say that some cousins in the larger branch won't be larger earners, marry into wealthier families or win the lottery. It is only an example to show how a conflict manager might look at a family system in conflict and recognize sibling or branch wealth disparity as a possible reason why that conflict exists.

When wealth disparity exists within a generation, it is important to understand how it developed. This is especially true when the wealth involved is shared or inherited because issues of fairness abound. When any stakeholder exerts influence over another from a position that the target of that influence sees as lacking in moral authority (i.e., unfair), that act will likely be seen as Disrespected Power and will likely trigger conflict.

New Wealth

Some families are fortunate to experience a significant liquidity event at some point in time. When families decide to sell their business, they may be catapulted into a very new set of economic circumstances. These stakeholders will likely face a crisis of identity. As these families try to figure out who they are with respect to their new circumstance of wealth, they will need to explore new values and goals that they have not yet had the opportunity to experience.

Stakeholders who are new to significant wealth will often need to change many of their advisory relationships. Relationships among family members may change as well. When stakeholders were tied together by an operating business, they needed to engage with each other and make decisions together. When the business is gone, what, if anything, will hold family relationships together? Restructuring the purpose of family when a structure that was historically important to the family is gone can cause stress and make conflict more likely.

In such an extreme state of flux, mistakes will be made. Values and goals may be highly variable – at least during the time that stakeholder identities are adapting to new economic circumstances. During these times, the likelihood that goals will be in opposition and values will be incompatible among family stakeholders will be higher.

Anticipating this, one client we worked with was hesitant to sell his company at a time when many advisors and other family stakeholders were urging him to do so based on changes in the industry. Worrying about the effect of a sale, he confided in us that he only saw significant downside if he went through with it. He worried about the effect of wealth disparity on his relationships with his siblings, who years ago had opted out of the business, as a sale would make him ten times wealthier than they. In addition, he worried that life as he knew it would change. He enjoyed being an executive in a company that employed hundreds of people in his community, solving problems in manufacturing, and managing his staff. He also worried about the effect of tremendous new wealth on his children and on his relationships with his friends and other family members whom he loved. He had plenty of money and enjoyed his life. Was it worth the risk?

As the example above illustrates, new wealth, while exciting, brings with it life changes. A conflict manager needs to be sensitive to the challenges and responsibilities that come from new wealth and help stakeholders to anticipate the effects of new wealth on families and to prepare for or manage their new situation.

Narcissism

Enterprising families can generally trace their economic success to the entrepreneurial efforts of a few individuals. These individuals believed in themselves and their ability to change the world (or their community, the industry, etc.). They believed that what they could do was better than what others could do, and was something that the world needed. They worked hard; differentiated their companies, products and services from competitors; pushed through obstacles that would have subdued others; and led others to follow their vision. This unstoppable self-confidence and ability to lead sometimes draws claims of narcissism from stakeholders who may not fare well under this leader's regime. The fact is that many of the traits required for being a successful entrepreneur have a degree of similarity to a personality trait that psychologists term "narcissism."

The word "narcissism" is rarely seen as positive. But without a healthy dose of narcissism, there would be far fewer successful entrepreneurs. In order to achieve the extraordinary, people must believe in their inherent extraordinary abilities or gifts. And so, we are taking the risk in this book to declare that productive narcissism, a term coined by psychologist and anthropologist Michael Maccoby in his book *The Productive Narcissist*, is not the enemy of family business — despite the fact that, as advisors, we hear the word "narcissist" thrown around frequently. Not only do we hear this word used derisively when stakeholders in conflict describe other stakeholders, but we even hear other consultants dismissing clients as narcissists to explain why they were not successful in a case.

When most people hear the word "narcissist," they immediately think of pathological narcissists who are self-centered, manipulative people who don't listen to others and who stop at nothing to get their way. Like it or not, these are characteristics attributable, in some measure, to many successful entrepreneurs.

A comparison to another malady that occurs frequently in family business is instructive. Evidence indicates that alcoholism is a problem that disproportionately impacts family businesses, and this will be discussed later in the chapter. One difference between alcoholism and narcissism is that there is no competitive advantage that comes from being a little bit drunk or a little bit addicted. However, there may be dramatic competitive advantage for an entrepreneur possessing characteristics that might be considered a little bit narcissistic.

The issue of productive narcissism in business leadership is not limited to the family business. After all, these characteristics are evidenced by many successful entrepreneurs of non-family businesses. The trouble with these behaviors in a family business is that they can be very destructive in the context of family – family at the office who must work with these leaders, and family at home that live with these leaders – especially when these behaviors become pathological.

In a family system, spouses and children need to be heard and acknowledged. One of the defining characteristics of narcissistic behavior is a diminished ability to acknowledge others. Productive narcissism at the office can, therefore, be destructive narcissism at home and it can have a devastating impact on the rising generation. Keep in mind, if the perceived victim of (productively) narcissistic leadership is a rising generation that may be less self-differentiated, even a reasonable level of productive narcissism may be perceived as damaging to these individuals.

An additional problem with productive narcissism is that it exists in a system that often allows it to get out of control. Business leaders are at the top of the hierarchical pyramid at the office. Subordinates defer to them and these leaders often have no independent accountability system to serve as a check for how their behavior impacts others. Like pouring gasoline on a fire, productive narcissism can become destructive narcissism over time in such circumstances.

It is also difficult to turn off "being the boss" when these stakeholders go home to spouses, children, brothers, sisters and cousins — where one needs to work as a team member and even take out the trash. We do not mean to imply here that all strong business leaders and successful entrepreneurs suffer from narcissistic personality disorder or that they have problematic relations with family members. We are only pointing out that the dichotomy between being the leader in the business system and a collaborator in the family system is sometimes difficult to manage. Productive narcissistic tendencies, so essential for business success, can leak over into family relationships, leading to conflict and dysfunction.

While much good can come from productive narcissism, there are a myriad of side effects that can occur. It is impossible to describe all the manifestations of these challenges that are seen in the family business system, but here are a few examples:

- Children often feel compelled to follow in Mom's or Dad's footsteps, devoting their careers to the company (often in vain) because that is the only way to get the acknowledgement that wasn't available to them in their formative years.
- Marriages can become dysfunctional and many end in divorce. Stress in the marriage can lead to insecurity in the children.
- Children who have been denied the positive role model of a nurturing mother or father may not have learned the skills needed to be a nurturing mother or father themselves, thus perpetuating the cycle.
- When the focus of family life is on the entrepreneurial parent, children can grow up without a strong sense of themselves and become insecure, targets for all sorts of peer pressure and abuse.
- In an attempt to recast their upbringing as positive, children might see truly destructive behavior as normal, and seek to replicate that behavior in their own relationships. Without the underlying skill sets, talents and experience of the parent, these behaviors prevent children and young adults from developing functional adult relationships and successful careers.

Unfortunately, there are few ways of dealing with a degree of narcissistic behavior that is perceived as problematic in an enterprising family system. When the behavior is extreme, and rises to a personality disorder, it is considered one of the most difficult conditions to treat. Some say that it is untreatable – primarily because the patient cannot achieve the perspective to see how their behavior impacts others. In these cases, it is the family and the employees that must adapt or establish healthy boundaries for themselves. This may mean that an option of a successful career in the family business is not possible for some stakeholders.

In cases where narcissism is productive, stakeholders should understand that this is a slippery slope. They must be ever-vigilant to establish checks and balances to prevent this behavior — behavior that should be celebrated rather than demonized — from going to the dark side. Exploring Personal and Structural Development options for this purpose is well advised – especially in the early stages of a family enterprise.

Entitlement

Growing up in an affluent family can be more challenging than it may seem. Children often are exposed to so much opportunity, and potentially relieved from so much responsibility, that it can be confusing and difficult to emerge with a strong sense of self and a realistic view of the world. To combat this, many affluent parents try extremely hard to keep their kids grounded, and they spend a lot of time trying to ensure that their values are connected to the traditional values that made their family strong.

Challenges are many for these families and there will be a certain percentage that, to use a baseball metaphor, woke up on third base and believe that they hit a triple.

There will also be those exposed to similar situations who withdraw and feel unworthy of the benefits they experience. They may actively rebel against this entitlement – in which case their behavior is still motivated by entitlement, but their behavior is opposite. Some may end up passive, unengaged in any meaningful or productive enterprise.

When so many of the needs expressed in Maslow's hierarchy are achieved just by being born, very affluent children can lose out on the character-building opportunities that go along with achieving these needs for themselves. It is a difficult task for a family to provide both the benefits of affluence and the opportunities for building character.

Parents sometimes insist upon their children engaging in the opportunities that they have worked so hard to provide. And while the children may be encouraged in some respects to forge their own paths, not going into the family business may be perceived as disloyal. Living within one's own means, when the family can provide significantly more, may be met with derision and seen as foolish.

An overarching problem that children of affluence face is that when they seek help, or express some of the psychological difficulties they may be having to their friends, they may not find much sympathy. Accordingly, young adults tend to stay within their affluent peer groups, who reinforce common values and understand the same challenges, thus missing the alternative views that might be beneficial for attaining perspective and growth.

Entitlement can also be understood in the context of narcissism. A child may feel unworthy when he or she "wakes up on third base." They may have a sense of guilt over what they have. As humans, we are all hardwired to survive and we innately try to make sense of our lives so that we can move forward. Feeling guilty and unworthy are negative emotions that hurt one's chances for survival. Instead, individuals may convince themselves that they are exceptional and, thus, worthy of their opportunity and position, even without having proven themselves. This false sense of power and confidence may be needed for the individual to make sense of their world. In this manner, entitlement can lead to narcissistic behaviors.

Families who manage entitlement well do so by instilling a sense of gratitude and responsibility in their rising generations. Some families insist upon rising generations "earning" their "gifts," but these efforts can often seem contrived and be counterproductive if not well thought through. When families proactively provide development opportunities for rising generations and build sensible, effective wealth integration strategies and structures, entitlement behavior can be minimized and rising generations can indeed become true stewards and productive managers of the wealth and opportunity that did not come directly from their own efforts.

Substance Abuse and Addiction

Many enterprising families are challenged by substance abuse and addiction at some point in their evolution. In many ways, life within an enterprising family can be the perfect storm for substance abuse to develop. When stress, opportunity, and lack of consequence or accountability combine, bad things can happen.

Running a business, or having significant financial responsibility is stressful in itself. But when it is in the context of a family enterprise, it can be even more stressful for many of the reasons outlined in this book. Stakeholders may be struggling with identity and conflict issues from which they seek escape through alcohol, prescription or illicit drug use, or even gambling and other compulsive behaviors.

In family enterprise, stakeholders in such stressful situations may not be part of a transparent, accountable system. Their last name and connections may shield them from the consequences of their behavior. Alcohol and other substances are widely available in both business and social circumstances, and the pressure to partake abounds. Business deals are closed over drinks, and social events for the privileged are sometimes fueled with energy boosting, mind-altering chemicals. And, it doesn't help that in many enterprising families, money is available and not an obstacle to finding such resources.

There are certainly many reasons why some people are more susceptible to addiction and substance abuse than others, including genetic predisposition, and this book is not intended to be a detailed study. Rather, it is only to point out that there are reasons why enterprising families should be particularly aware of this threat.

Neuroscience

In Chapter 2 we discussed the nature of identity-based conflict. Research shows that individuals do not feel "safe" until they are confident that their identity is recognized, acknowledged and respected. Personal growth and the ability to negotiate cannot happen when one's identity is perceived to be under threat.

Studying what happens in the brain, Dr. Daniel J. Siegel explains in his book, *Mindsight: The New Science of Personal Transformation*, that when individuals are in a reasonably stress-free state, brain activity is concentrated in the prefrontal lobe, allowing the individual to be open to creative, rational thinking. When experiencing conflict, however, the limbic part of the brain is activated, putting people into a reactive state where they are unable to process new information or think and act rationally.

Accordingly, when individuals feel that their identity is threatened, the fight-flight-or-freeze part of the brain, the amygdala, hijacks their ability to think rationally and their capacity for productive communication is lost. For

> Identity issues are not negotiable – you can't negotiate who you are, and you can't negotiate your belief and values systems. The more that your values and beliefs are threatened, the more tightly you will hold on to them.

us as a species, fight-flight-or-freeze is a good and necessary thing for survival. At the office or at a family event, however, it may not be so beneficial, and this may explain why family business stakeholders can become so deeply entrenched in their positions.

Family business conflict involves issues that are core to each stakeholder's identity and these identity issues are not negotiable – you can't negotiate who you are, and you can't negotiate your belief and values systems. Instead, the more that your values and beliefs are threatened, the more tightly you will hold on to them.

Too often advisors to family business do not understand this. They attempt to force negotiations, admonishing stakeholders to "leave emotion out of the room." Those emotions are connected to stakeholder identity and when they are told, in so many words, that their identity is just getting in the way, their positions harden and their ability to hear and think rationally is compromised.

When stakeholders and their advisors understand that there is a neuroscientific reason for some of the less-than-rational behaviors that they experience in the family business system, they can begin to become open to alternative approaches for managing conflict. By acknowledging that the issues at hand are based in deep-seated perceptions of identity, stakeholders can take a more nuanced approach to managing conflict through the various personal and structural development efforts described in this book.

Summary
- The psychology of enterprising family systems is in some respects different from that of non-enterprising family systems. Individual stakeholders face both opportunities and challenges from being part of an enterprising family.
- Bowen Family Systems Theory is a useful framework to understand many of the psychological and emotional challenges faced by members of enterprising families.
- Differentiation of self and enmeshment are key concepts that influence stakeholders of family enterprise.
- Narcissism, often a helpful characteristic of a successful entrepreneur, can have a significant negative effect on the development of an enterprising family.

- Family enterprise can create the perfect storm for substance abuse and addiction problems.
- Neuroscience explains some of what is at play in the brain of a stakeholder grappling with identity-based conflict.

Chapter 11

Conclusion

Peace is not absence of conflict, it is the ability to handle conflict by peaceful means.
— Ronald Reagan

The Conflict Equation is a proven methodology that illustrates the relationships between the different components at play in the family business system at any given time, and through that identification, indicates what is needed to manage overall conflict.

The Conflict Equation is a roadmap for understanding conflict in any individual family business system. Once understood, it can be used to manage that conflict. It is not an equation that needs to be solved, nor is the goal to drive the equation to zero (i.e., to have Conflict = zero). It would be easy to drive the equation to zero by reducing Interdependence to zero through severing family contact and closing or selling the business to have everyone go their separate ways. While this certainly is an option, it likely is not the preferred route. How empty would our lives be if we sought the easy solution to our problems?

Conflict is inescapable in family enterprise. It is built into the very fabric of the system. It is the immune system of family enterprise that tells us what isn't functioning well so we can address it. If appropriately managed, conflict can be held in check and the system can evolve productively over time. If unaddressed or dealt with poorly, however, conflict can destroy the system.

Using *The Conflict Equation* to deconstruct conflict and to develop strategies to manage conflict will help drive all stakeholders to achieve their goals while preserving their values. When their shared goals are the advancement of business, wealth and family members, and their shared values speak to family harmony, value creation and generosity, simply managing conflict can have an enormous impact on families and their enterprise.

Best Practices for the Family Business

The study of family business has no shortage of so-called "best practices." Best practices are structures, processes and policies that have been employed by successful companies in the past. Many of these best practices make sense intuitively. However, *even the best "best practice" is likely to work against the interests of at least some of the stakeholders in a family enterprise.* The unintended consequence of trying to employ any best practice may very well be increased conflict. But, reliance on so-called best practices has additional shortcomings.

> Even the best "best practice" is likely to work against the interests of at least some of the stakeholders in a family enterprise.

There is an important difference between correlation and causality. The fact that a particular practice is common among many successful family businesses may imply that it is indeed a practice that *causes* that enterprise to be successful – at least in part. However, it could also be that just as many families who employ that particular practice fail.

The Conflict Equation is a qualitative tool and framework for considering all best practices. Rather than prescribing a specific solution simply because that solution worked for other organizations, *The Conflict Equation* guides the conflict manager to consider the most appropriate remedies for a specific reason for, or trigger of, conflict. It also identifies opportunities for developing stakeholders and their organizations, for which some best practices may be useful.

Certainly, the success or failure of a family enterprise is due to many factors. But only when conflict is managed can families focus on long-term success strategies for both the family and its enterprise. Only when conflict is managed well can stakeholders develop creative solutions that work, and successfully implement productive changes.

Lay a Strong Foundation

Best practices are certainly useful, however. They offer a rich landscape of ideas and are often supported by anecdotal evidence and statistics to back them up. One useful way to think about best practices is to consider the analogy of building a stone foundation wall.

Stones are irregularly shaped, so there is an art to making a strong stone wall. Each stone is selected and arranged with care and attention to its particular shape and qualities. Occasionally, the mason chisels a stone to fit it in place. In addition to good strong stones of the right shape and size, however, the right mortar must be used. Each stone is surrounded by mortar and, combined, they make the foundation solid enough to build upon. The mortar must be of the right mixture so that it will adhere to the types of stone chosen. The mortar must also be able to survive through many seasons and environmental challenges.

Think of these stones as best practices. As business leaders build the foundation of their business, they incorporate a variety of best practices – as well as creative solutions to problems and challenges that arise. If these policies, structures and procedures make up the foundation of the business, effective conflict management is the mortar that holds the foundation together and keeps the company strong. Well-designed conflict management approaches should surround even the best "best practice." Conflict management is what connects every best practice, creative solution and work-around, to build a solid foundation for the company that will weather the storms of the challenges ahead.

There is certainly a place for the deductive, or best-practice approach. Every conflict manager should be aware of the best practices for the systems they work with. The conflict manager needs to consider the widest palette of interventions in order to be of highest service to their client. However, the application of each best practice should be dictated by the specific needs of the system, not simply because a given practice has worked in the past, most of the time, for other organizations.

Beginning Your Journey

Whether you are a stakeholder in a family business, an advisor to a family business, a family member within a wealthy family, or a teacher of family business theory, we hope this book has resonated with you. We have applied *The Conflict Equation* approach for deconstructing conflict with many families, even those in active litigation, and we have seen how transformative it can be. Now, it's your turn.

If you are reading this book, you likely have the opportunity to influence the family enterprise systems you are involved with. If you are a family business stakeholder, use the concepts in this book to first understand your own behaviors and expectations. Learn how conflict is influenced by your behavior and find opportunities to develop yourself and the organizations in which you participate. Identify opportunities to release blame over Historical Impasse. And, above all, find opportunities to build your Family Factor. Nothing will have more of an impact for good.

If you are an advisor to family businesses or to families of wealth, consider the big picture by using the Stakeholder Map. Be collaborative. Use *The Conflict Equation* to identify areas of development needed by the family and its enterprise that require a team of collaborative professionals, and build that team. Understand the limitations of your own profession in helping clients manage conflict, and reach out to other professionals who understand families and who can serve them well as part of a team.

If you practice a profession that traditionally requires you to serve a single stakeholder (such as an attorney, psychologist, or financial planner), understand that your client may be best served by broadening the definition of "who the client is." Enterprising family stakeholders are part of a system that cannot be understood, treated or advised in isolation.

Finally, a special note to litigators: This book is not very kind regarding litigation as an option for family business stakeholders in conflict. In most cases, litigation will be considered additional Disrespected Power and trigger increased conflict. But, litigation is sometimes necessary and unavoidable. When large sums are involved, the financial cost of litigation may not be a discouraging factor. However, the human cost of litigation is something that should always be considered. When families reach out to you to have their day in court, consider including someone in the process who understands the concepts laid out in this book. Litigation does not have to destroy families. Include someone on the team who can work alongside you to keep the process from causing irreparable damage, needlessly ruining family relationships. Remember that the charge to move forward only with the client's *informed consent* requires that the client be informed of the costs, uncertainties and risks inherent in the litigation process. Helping clients avoid costly litigation when other alternatives exist may not be as lucrative, but it is good business and, in the long run, will be a competitive edge for litigators and their firms.

A Word About Family Business Consultancy

There are no standards, no licenses required, and no regulations regarding the practice of family business consultancy. Good family business consultancy requires facility in psychology and family systems as well as law, business, and conflict management. It is difficult to be an expert in all these areas, and, for that reason a team approach is useful. Each team member, however, should have exposure to each of these disciplines so that they speak a common language and know when to defer to others and when to assert their expertise and insight.

The Conflict Equation framework described in this book can serve as the common language for such a consulting team. It is intended to be used as a framework for the assessment process and a roadmap for developing plans and options. Properly used, *The Conflict Equation* identifies the collaborative team needed to develop each stakeholder, each stakeholder group, and the structures that connect them.

Having experience as a family business stakeholder can provide great insight into client situations. However, this is not a requirement for being a good family business consultant. Family business stakeholders wanting to become consultants need to go through the process of understanding their family business history so that they do not project their experience onto client situations. Working as a team can help leverage the insights that come from having been a stakeholder in family business, while also providing balance.

Deconstructing Conflict

The media routinely cover scandalous stories of conflict in families over business, shared wealth, and power. Large sums are claimed as recompense for all manner of betrayal and insult. It is easy to dismiss these as stories of greed and to focus on the money involved. It is important to understand, however, that more often than not, stakeholders are not really fighting about the money or the power. Rather, money and power are simply representative of deeper issues. These battles are really about identity, being respected, and being acknowledged. In addition, what may start out as a minor skirmish is exacerbated by the inherently conflictual systems that define family enterprise.

Deconstructing conflict is the best way to understand what really is at play when families own or work together and experience the challenges of conflict inherent in these systems. It is only through unpacking these situations into their component parts that conflict can be managed and family business systems can move forward successfully.

Epilogue

When human beings live together, conflict is inevitable. War is not.
— *Daisaku Ikeda*

So, where do we go from here? Family business is the perfect crucible for understanding systemic, identity-based conflict, when continuing relationships matter. This means that the methodology for deconstructing conflict presented in this book can be applied to other kinds of conflict, such as ethnic, religious, political and cultural conflicts. Just as families have uniquely permanent relationships, so too do citizens in neighboring countries, diverse religious followers in pluralistic societies, and residents in culturally diverse school districts.

Like families, ethnic, religious and political groups carry with them long historical narratives that shape their perception of the fairness or unfairness of their plight. *The Conflict Equation* can be adapted to these situations because it is a methodology, not a best practice. Each of these types of groups holds some power that may or may not be disrespected by others; each has reasons for conflict. While they don't have a Family Factor™, they do have a Relationship Factor™ that incorporates their shared history, shared vision for the future, and level of trust. As in the family business context, if this component can be increased, it can lower the level of overall conflict and make the system more resilient in the face of change.

So much of international conflict management is based on dispute resolution techniques, such as negotiation and force (i.e., war). Opponents on the international stage argue over identity-based issues that, as we have discussed in this book, are not negotiable. Conflicts are treated as disputes, rather than systemic conflicts that demand more than simple dispute resolution approaches. Rather than trying to force a resolution to intractable conflict, or endlessly trying to negotiate the unnegotiable, we believe that the concepts in this book can be fully applied to these situations. Doing so would lead to developmental approaches, not force or negotiation alone, and could lead to successful outcomes for all involved.

We hope this book begins a new approach to thinking rationally about how to manage conflict in situations where identity-based conflict is at play and where important continuing relationships hang in the balance.

The Conflict Equation

$$C_t \propto \frac{ID \times DP \times (OG + IV + HI)}{FF \times (SD + PD + DR + RB)} + XF$$

C_t = Conflict over Time
$\propto$ = is proportional to
ID = Interdependence
OG = Opposing Goals
IV = Incompatible Values
HI = Historical Impasse
DP = Disrespected Power
FF = Family Factor
      Shared History, Trust,
      Shared Vision
XF = External Factors
SD = Structural Development
PD = Personal Development
DR = Dispute Resolution
RB = Releasing Blame

Appendix

The Twelve Components of the Conflict Equation

The Conflict Equation lays out a roadmap for data collection and investigation. Each of the twelve Components of the equation is a data point and the following tools hold the answers:

Solving for C = Conflict:

> Can be Active (fighting) or Passive (being stuck)
> Is systemic, not isolatable disputes, though individual disputes may exist as part of the systemic conflict
> Is identity-based

1. **ID – Interdependence:** What levels of interdependence exist within the Family Enterprise System?
    a. Stakeholder Map shows the various systems in which stakeholders "live."
    b. Genogram depicts the family connections in detail.
    c. Org-Chart shows the working relationships among stakeholders.
    d. Estate Plan and other documents show the current and future ownership and control relationships, and lays out the trustee/beneficiary relationships.
    e. Can the system be developed to tolerate greater interdependence?
    f. Does the system, after sufficient analysis and attempts at intervention, require interdependence to be changed or reduced? How might that be accomplished?

2. **DP – Disrespected Power:** Who holds power and how do they use power?
    a. Org-chart
    b. Job descriptions and related policies

    c.   Ownership structure and shareholder agreements

    d.   Governance structure and by-laws

    e.   The importance of family rank

    f.   Stories and examples of the use of power determined through personal interviews and work samples

    g.   Looking at the system through the lens of the five types of power – who can direct, punish, reward, connect, influence?

3. **OG – Opposing Goals**

    a.   Personal interviews can identify individual's goals as they relate to the business and family issues at hand.

    b.   A comparative review of the system-wide interviews can identify where those individual goals are in opposition to the goals of other stakeholders.

    c.   What opposing goals might respond to bargaining?

    d.   What opposing goals might respond to personal development such as education and trust building?

4. **IV – Incompatible Values**

    a.   Personal interviews can identify individual's relevant values as they relate to the business and family issues at hand.

    b.   A comparative review of the system-wide interviews can identify where those individual values are incompatible with the values of other stakeholders.

    c.   Investigating shared and individual philanthropy can indicate values alignment.

    d.   What incompatible values might respond to personal development, such as building empathy and experiential learning?

5. **HI – Historical Impasse**

    a.   Personal interviews can identify past hurts and grudges held by individual stakeholders.

    b.   A comparative review of the system-wide interviews can identify common themes and misperceptions. Can these be cleared up through discussion or forensic analysis?

    c.   What historical impasses might respond to exercises in forgiveness and personal development, such as trust and empathy building?

6. **FF – Family Factor:** Does this family have a vision for being family? Do they spend time together? Do they invest in family capital?
   a. FF is a combination of Shared History, Trust and Shared Vision for being family.
   b. Personal interviews can reveal levels of trust, shared history and vision for being family in the future.
   c. Asset analysis can begin conversations about family boats, vacation homes, and vacations.
   d. Evaluating the insurance portfolio can determine if the family has thought through their resilience going forward.
   e. Looking at the investment portfolio of each stakeholder can reveal levels of transparency, investment in human capital, and interest in sharing wealth and opportunity.
   f. Can the Family Factor be improved through trust-building exercises?
   g. Can the Family Factor be improved through development of a shared vision of what being family will mean in the future?
   h. Can revisiting and recasting the past through a new perspective and new information improve the Family Factor?

7. **SD – Structural Development:** Improving SD can reduce conflict.
   a. Is there an appropriate level of professional systems in place? Is there an ERP system, for example, and should there be?
   b. Are the organizational structure, job descriptions and policies clear, unambiguous, appropriate and accurate?
   c. Is corporate governance sufficiently developed as appropriate for the business and its ownership circumstances?
   d. Is there a process flowchart or ISO Manual that clearly details how things are done and how information flows in the system?
   e. Are there clear compensation policies that comport with industry norms?
   f. Is there a review process and a set of accountability standards for family and non-family employees that works well?

g. Is there an exit strategy for those who wish to change their position in the system?

h. Are advisors conflicted?

i. Are agreements and policies clearly articulated and apparent to all?

j. Would formal structure within the family, such as a family council or family website, provide needed focus, commitment and communication?

8. **PD – Personal Development**

a. Are all stakeholders properly trained, educated and skilled for the roles they perform, or desire to perform, in the family enterprise system?

b. Are there opportunities for improving trust and empathy?

c. Have individual interviews identified the need for psychological intervention?

d. Have individual interviews identified the need for substance abuse intervention?

e. Would personal or group coaching help stakeholders perform better?

f. Would outplacement services help individuals transition?

g. Can family functioning improve through education and experiential learning?

9. **DR – Dispute Resolution**

a. Are there individual disputes that need to be addressed and could be addressed by mediation or direct negotiation?

b. Can opposing goals be negotiated?

c. Can power be negotiated?

d. Can specific behaviors be negotiated?

10. **RB – Releasing Blame**

a. Are there historical impasses, and individuals who have experienced these impasses, that would respond to a proactive process for achieving forgiveness or acceptance?

b. Are there misperceptions that could be cleared up to resolve historical impasses?

c. Can faith-based interventions help stakeholders move beyond difficult pasts?

11. **XF – External Factors**
    a. What is going on in the market that might increase stress, anxiety, and conflict in the system?
    b. What is going on in the economy?
    c. What is going on in the regulatory system?
    d. What is going on with world politics?

12. **Time**
    a. What interventions and system characteristics require significant time to have impact or to develop?
    b. Does the impact of timing change the order or priority of interventions?
    c. How will the system develop over time as estate plans trigger, companies mature, and families develop?
    d. Is the system prepared for a crisis? What type of preparation would be useful?

Bibliography

Beyond Conflict (report authors Melinda Burrell and Judy Barsalou). "Neuroscience and Peacebuilding: Reframing How We Think About Conflict and Prejudice." January 2015. http://www.beyondconflictint.org/2014/wp-content/uploads/2015/10/Neuroscience-and-Peacebuilding_v1.pdf

Fisher, Roger, and William Ury. *Getting to Yes: Negotiating Agreement Without Giving In.* Penguin Group, 1981; most recent edition 2011)

French, John R. P., and Bertrand Raven. "The Bases of Social Power," in *Group Dynamics*, D. Cartwright and A. Zander, editors. New York: Harper & Row, 1959.

Gilbert, Roberta, M. *The Eight Concepts of Bowen Theory.* Leading Systems Press, 2006.

Grubman, James. *Strangers in Paradise: How Families Adapt to Wealth Across Generations.* Family Wealth Consulting, 2013.

Kachaner, Nicolas, George Stalk, Jr., and Alain Bloch. "What You Can Learn from Family Business" Harvard Business Review, November 2012. https://hbr.org/2012/11/what-you-can-learn-from-family-business

McGoldrick, Monica and Gerson, Randy. *Genograms in Family Assessment.* W.W. Norton & Company, 1986.

Papero, Daniel V. (with Foreword by Dr. Murray Bowen). *Bowen Family Systems Theory.* Pearson, 1990.

Phillips, Timothy, and Mary Albon, Ina Breuer, and David Taffel, editors. *Beyond Conflict: 20 Years of Putting Experience to Work for Peace.* Brideswell Books, 2013.

Siegel, Daniel J. *Mindsight: The New Science of Personal Transformation.* Bantam, 2009.

Abrahms-Spring, Janis. *How Can I Forgive You? The Courage to Forgive, the Freedom Not To.* HarperCollins Publishers, 2004.

Toman, Walter. *Family Constellation: Its Effects on Personality and Social Behavior.* Springer Publishing Company, 1992.

Wilmot, William, and Joyce Hocker. *Interpersonal Conflict*, 9th edition. McGraw-Hill Higher Education, 2013.

About the Authors

Doug Baumoel has spent the majority of his career in and around family businesses, having served as the second-generation leader in his own family's business and holding executive posts in other family-operated companies both in the US and abroad. Widely respected for his insights on leadership, governance, succession and conflict management in family enterprise, he writes and speaks extensively, and is the Founding Partner of Continuity LLC, a global firm working with family businesses and their stakeholders. Educated in engineering at Cornell and with an MBA from Wharton, he holds a number of distinctions, including Fellow of the National Association of Corporate Directors and the Family Firm Institute.

Blair Trippe is an experienced negotiator, mediator, and family business consultant. As a co-creator of the specialized field of elder mediation, she transformed the practice of helping adult siblings manage the issues confronting aging family members. With a background that includes executive posts on Wall Street and in other corporate settings, she is the Managing Partner of Continuity LLC and has served on numerous boards. Her grasp of family enterprise systems has garnered the trust of a wide range of family business executives, board members, and other stakeholders. She earned an MBA at Northwestern's Kellogg School, studied psychology at Connecticut College, and earned certificates in negotiation and mediation through the Program on Negotiation at Harvard University.

Notes

Made in the USA
Lexington, KY
01 July 2017